Grains of Sand

Grains of Sand

Benson M. Karanja

Mall Publishing Co.

THE PRINTED WORD THE PLANTED SEED

HIGHLAND PARK, ILLINOIS

Printed in the United States of America

Published by:
Mall Publishing Company
641 Homewood Avenue
Highland Park, Illinois 60035
Toll Free: 1-877-203-2453
E-mail: info@mallpublishing.biz
Website: www.mallpublishing.biz

Book Design by Marlon B. Villadiego
Cover Design by Andrew Ostrowski

ISBN 1-934165-05-0

For licensing / copyright information, for additional copies or for use in specialized settings contact:

Dr. Benson M. Karanja

892 Berne Street
Atlanta, GA 30316
Office: 404-627-2681
Fax: 404-627-0702
benson.karanja@beulah.org
www.beulah.org

Dedication . . . .

I dedicate this book to my wife, Esther,

my three children, Robinson, Juliet, and Peter

who have always been there for me, my father,

the late Robinson Karanja, who pointed me in the right

direction and my mother, the late Harriet Karanja

who believed in me and believed that I was on a mission.

. . . .

Table of Contents . . . .

. . . .

Acknowledgement . . . .

T his book views the grace of God at work. This grace and love of God is expressed and manifested through those who support me, care for me, and stand with me. Among them is my lovely wife Esther, who has been my number one cheerleader and my driving force through the years. Her patience is second to none. My gratitude goes also to my children Robinson, Juliet, and Peter. They are indeed blessings from God.

I am grateful to Dr. Samuel Chand, my predecessor, who encouraged me to be all that I could be. He gave me a platform to exercise my leadership skills. He is my friend and I will be forever grateful to him.

I cannot forget my team players at Beulah Heights Bible College; they form the best team in the world. They have made my work easier and productive. I especially thank my able Executive Assistant, Alvita Thompson.

I appreciate my Pastor, Dr. Scott Weimer, who always has time to listen. His spiritual guidance has been constant. I also appreciate Cecil Murphy for working on my initial draft, Angie Baird who reviewed my initial draft, and Jacquelyn Armstrong, who added finishing touches.

But most of all, I thank God for His grace that has spread like a sheltering blanket over me, my family, and my ministry.

Many people have shaped my life and encouraged me through my journey. It is impossible to mention them all, but I'm so grateful for their love and friendship.

Foreword . . . .

W hat you hold in your hand is no ordinary book. Reading it is likely to be a life-altering experience. It is the gut-wrenching and inspiring personal story of Benson Karanja, an African who came to America as a student and rose through poverty and prejudice to embrace his divinely determined destiny. You cannot read this amazing account without being freshly reminded of how God works to bring us through all adversities to fulfill His special purposes for us. Importantly as well, this book forces us to take a careful look into our own hearts and come to grips with our own attitudes.

This is a fascinating saga of the incredible journey of a boy born in the Kikuyu tribe on a farm, in a portion of East Africa that was soon to become the independent nation of Kenya. It tells of early prophecies spoken by village elders that were fulfilled as he grew up to become a successful businessman, helping hundreds of families become productive farmers. Fulfillment continued as he first traveled to Israel on behalf of a large Kenyan farming association to study the agricultural methods of the Israelis. After that experience, he traveled to America as a representative of Kenyan Christian business leadership at a large international event. This story-book saga also relates the surprising chain of events which led Benson Karanja to know that God wanted him to attend a Bible college in America.

You cannot help but stand in awe at the grace of God that sustained Benson Karanja as he moved to Atlanta to attend Bible college and met with unexpected racial prejudice and selective mistreatment of himself and his family. After years of financial success, he found himself, his wife, and three children cramped into a run-down one-bedroom college apartment, performing janitorial work and struggling just to find food for the family each day. Your heart will feel his pain as he suffered rejection for the first time as a black man, as he was shunned by a local church and as his appeals for help were brushed off by several U.S. missionaries he knew in Africa. But as you follow his story, you will be inspired by his valiant example of faith in God, patience, endurance, and determined achievement. Above all, you will be impressed with the greatness of a Christ-like heart that harbors no resentment – only understanding and forgiveness.

Dr. Benson Karanja is a patiently quiet, soft-spoken man with obvious inner spiritual strength and a genuine interest in others. I first became acquainted with him in 1993, when I joined the faculty of Beulah Heights Bible College in Atlanta. At the time, he held the newly created position of Fiscal Officer for the college. While in this full-time capacity, he volunteered in the college library, helping it meet accreditation standards. At the time I met him, he also worked part-time at a local children's hospital as a behavioral specialist. He had precious little spare time, but made time to have a quick lunch with me several times that first year. I remember how greatly I appreciated his effort to make me feel welcome on the campus.

Our wives became good friends as well, and we enjoyed having Benson and Esther come for dinner in our home. On several occasions my wife Jackie and I attended North Avenue Presbyterian Church with the Karanjas. Although I could sense in my spirit that Benson was headed for much greater things, I had no idea in those days that he would one day take the helm as president of our college. We continued to work together in various aspects of college life, and even led mission teams together to his native home, Kenya and also to South Africa. I observed with awe the respect with which Benson was received in Africa. He was admired as an African who had found success and recognition in the United States. In Kenya, Benson and I, along with our mission team, found ourselves invited to have breakfast with President Moi at his summer home near Nakuru.

Benson Karanja continued to advance at the college and was named as Vice President in charge of Student Affairs. At the same time, he went back to school at Clarke Atlanta University and added a Master of Library Science Degree to the Master of Business Administration he had recently earned at Brenau University. An incredibly focused person, he managed to serve with excellence in his full-time work at the college and at the same time complete both degrees. I knew what a difficult struggle he and his family were going through, since there was once a similar season in my own life. But I never heard him complain – not once. He was always in good humor and took time to encourage me.

Dr. Benson Karanja is on an amazing journey. I have watched as God continued to mold his character and equip him with valuable experience. At North Avenue Presbyterian Church, he became President of the huge International Sunday School Class. He was sent out on several short term missions in various countries overseas. Soon after I met him, I learned that he was previously named to the missions committee that oversaw the expenditure of hundreds of thousands of dollars annually. Later, I saw him rise to leadership in two accrediting associations for U.S. colleges. In 2004, he was named as the new President of Beulah Heights Bible College.

He is now president of the very same college where he began as an unknown international student, working as a janitor desperately struggling to support his wife and three children. He is profoundly respected by all students, and especially so by the growing body of international students. They sense his genuine compassion for them, and recognize his commitment to make their experience as students at Beulah Heights Bible College a far happier one than his own. Unchanged by success, Karanja models integrity as he continues to be the same humble, friendly person I first met in 1993.

Dr. Karanja's leadership style is practical. He has brought the school onto a much sounder financial footing, building cash reserves for the first time in its history. His leadership style is relational. He knows each member of the BHBC team by name, and takes moments each day to greet and chat with everyone he passes during the day. His leadership style is built upon a work ethic. He is committed to excellence and with diligence. He routinely arrives at his office or to a first appointment by 7:00 A.M. His leadership style is visionary. With great clarity of vision he has defined new objectives for the college, making plans to bring it to university status in the near future. He envisions a new era for the historic old school, one in which it will be known worldwide as Beulah Heights University, offering a graduate program in Biblical Studies and Leadership and Administration. Partnering relationships with other institutions overseas are being hammered out in preliminary stages. The entire college obviously is moving quickly now toward a higher destiny spurred on by Dr. Karanja's visionary leadership.

It is highly evident to those who know Benson Karanja that God has bestowed unusual grace upon him. He continues to enjoy amazing favor in influential circles of spiritual, educational and financial leaders, not only in Atlanta but across America. This is an unfinished story with many chapters yet to be written as this man walks out his divinely ordained destiny in humility and consecration. Yet, here in

---

Grains of Sand

the story of his life thus far, Dr. Karanja shares priceless candid insights into how we all ought to live out our own life purposes. You will be blessed, as I have been, to read this wonderful testimony to the power of Christ that overcomes all adversity and turns it into blessing.

Doug Chatham, Ph.D., D.Min.
Professor of Biblical Studies
Beulah Heights Bible College
Atlanta, Georgia

xvi

Introduction . . . .

P eople sometimes ask why I went to Beulah Heights Bible College (BHBC) in Atlanta, Georgia. I was a successful businessman in Nakuru, Kenya; I was a member of the country club; I regularly socialized with the leading politicians and business people of the country. Why would I give up this lifestyle to become a student in a far-away country? Why would I leave a substantial business and take a job that paid $3.25 per hour?

The change in salary and respected lifestyle were not the only difficult challenges I faced. When I became a student at BHBC, I encountered racism and prejudice. My heart did not want to believe this could be true. Yet, I quickly understood the personal pain involved when people practice such attitudes and behavior. Some of it was open. Most of it manifested subtly. Judgments were made about me before people got to know me. An environment existed that fostered the concept of race superiority.

Shortly after enrolling as a student, I applied to become a member of a local church on campus. I patiently waited for a response. Three years later, an official of the church informed me that my membership application was lost. He provided no other explanation. No one offered me a new application. Yet for some reason, I did not leave. My family and I continued to attend services regularly for two more years. At times, I feel that perhaps I imposed an injustice

1

upon my family. To continue to worship at that church was a mistake but God still used the experience to prepare me for His plan.

Eventually, I became the Fiscal Officer in the Federal Financial Aid Department at the college. I was the first black person ever to be hired as an administrative staff person. I was the first black person ever to have an office at the college. Becoming an office employee was monumental. I had to prove myself and earn the trust of my co-workers. With my background in business, I knew I was capable of doing the job and any assignment that would be given to me despite the issues I faced. After several months, I finally had something to sit on instead of a hard, plastic chair. Having no telephone on my desk, presented me with yet another challenge. It became very difficult to do my work. However, I persevered in the face of these challenging situations.

I remember when the college administrators made the decision to purchase a fax machine. Financially, the college struggled in my early years as a student, as well as when I first became a staff member. To purchase a fax machine was a major decision and viewed as a great technological advancement. After some usage observations, the administrators held a staff meeting to discuss how the machine operated, who had permission to utilize this tool, and what acceptable college-related and business-related material could be sent and received.

As I heard the acceptable usage policies explained, it became apparent that the rules were for me. I had applied for my green card, which resulted in the need for occasional communication with my lawyer via the fax machine. I was also completing my graduate degree and had a great need for convenient correspondence to my professors. I had used the newly purchased fax machine. Receiving a fax required using paper and ink. Employees paid for paper and ink if they received a fax for personal business. Few could understand that my continued educational pursuit would benefit the college.

This is not a book to discuss the terrible ways people treated me. Rather, it is a book about God's grace, God's destiny, and God's power to produce perseverance, patience, and faith. It is about walking through darkness and trusting God completely—even when life does not make sense.

Although insulted, I stayed at Beulah Heights.

Although treated with contempt, I stayed at Beulah Heights.

Although two international corporations offered me jobs, I stayed at Beulah Heights.

Although I could have transferred to another college, I stayed at Beulah Heights.

"Why? Why would you go through all that?" a friend asked.

I am ready to explain why I stayed at Beulah Heights Bible College. I knew—even in 1987—that I would become a part of its history. When only 80 students comprised the total semester enrollment (mostly evening students), I was a member of the student body. When the college first began to seek accreditation, I was a member of the student body. When finances became very limited due to a drop in enrollment and the administration considered closing the college, I remained. When I had opportunities to leave for better-paying positions, I remained. When enrollment swelled to over 600 students, as a part of the administration, I rejoiced at what God had done.

During those years of hardship and problems, I believed God sent me to Beulah Heights Bible College for a reason. And the reason was beyond me. God used my circumstances to prepare me for something greater than I could envision. God had a much greater plan. I had to hope for the future and really believe that my uncomfortable circumstances were only temporary. God worked in ways that I could not have imagined.

Beginning in Kenya

E ven today, most westerners do not know much about the Kenya of my childhood. I was born on April 5, 1953, when our country was still a decade away from independence from England. The countries of Kenya, Uganda, and Tanganyika (later merged with the island of Zanzibar to become Tanzania) were known as East Africa with about thirty million people. Kenya was the last of the three countries to gain independence.

I am a Kikuyu, a member of the largest tribe in Kenya. I was born near Nakuru, the center of some of the richest farmland in Africa. It was known as Colonial White Highlands. Nakuru is in the Great Rift Valley, which starts in the country of Jordan, and goes through East Africa, down the coast, and ends somewhere in Mozambique. Lord Dalemare owned property in that location. His son still owns a huge farm south of Nairobi where the movie, *Out of Africa,* was filmed.

I was brought up at Gikammeh farm named after hyraxes, small furry animals that scratched their heads off every night from the trees. The farm was owned by an extended family of the British royal family named Jos and Nellie Grant, distant cousins of the Duke of York, and the parents of Elspeth Huxley, a well known author. Her works include, *White Man's Country (1935), Red Strangers (1939), The Sorcerer's Apprentice (1948), Forks and Hope (1964), Pioneer's Scrapbook (1980), Nellie: Letters from Africa (1981), Last Days in Eden (1984), and Out in Mid Day Sun (1985).* Her most famous book is *The Flame Trees of Thika.* Years ago, television network ABC made a successful mini-series based on the book. She mentions me as well as my family in her book, *Out in Mid Day Sun.* The farm lay on the margin of aboriginal forest, which was full of tall, majestic cedar with fluted bark, festooned with gray beards of lichen, and wild olives with twisted trunks and random branches.

I was ten years old when the British government granted independence to our country on December 7, 1963. It was a remarkable night. I remember the celebrations and the joy when we knew we were free. At midnight, the British flag came down. The Kenyan flag went up. Children, black and white, held hands playing together. We were equal. We celebrated together. Slavery disappeared like melting snow.

I remember until that time, every woman in the village had to work on the farm. They received twenty-five cents per day. But on our first day of freedom, they refused to go to work. We had choices. Each one of us were free to make our own decisions.

Worship experiences also changed. Black and white people began worshipping God together. Skin color was not an issue. Worshipping together was natural. Arriving in the United States, I could not understand the racism and prejudice that existed—especially in the Body of Christ. To find that in many areas people of different races would not worship together or were not welcome to worship together left me puzzled. My family and I eventually understood the pain of this reality.

By the time of Kenya's independence, the government had bought or taken over much of the area referred to as the white highlands, the farming community reserved for European white settlers. It is the most fertile land in Kenya. Until then, no African was permitted to own any property. Africans could be a worker for the government or a servant. But they were not permitted to own land. Owning property became difficult due to economic status. Few Kenyans had money. Wealth and economic status still separate many people.

Most Europeans left after December 7, 1963. Some went to South Africa. Others moved to Southern Rhodesia (Zimbabwe) and Portugal. Many returned to their own countries. Some stayed and became Kenyan as myself.

Instead of returning to England, however, Nellie Grant moved to Portugal. Her daughter, Elspeth, said that she

7

could not survive the winter in England.

• • • • •

Our family had lived on the Huxley farm as squatters. As squatters, the head of each family was given a piece of land, as a rule, about two or three acres. There he built his hut and his family grew their crops. In return, the head of the family was supposed to sign a contract to work for the master for life at a very low wage. For some reason, which I did not know at the time, we only had one acre of land. I came to realize later that my father had refused to sign the contract. I also found out that it was against the law for Africans to own animals. But, we did for a while. I remember in 1959 the police came around to see if contracts had been signed. Since my father was a cook, he found out about their coming ahead of time. He brought someone in to clean up after our animals. He had to have six goats killed. He had dirt brought in to cover the evidence of animals on our land. After this incident, we never kept animals again.

My father worked on that farm for fifty years. From the time he was just a small boy, he worked as a cook's helper in the farm kitchen. His name was Karanja, but as a child, he was called Toto Kanoi (Kitchen boy) by the Europeans. The Swahili word for child is mtoto, but the Europeans shortened it to Toto. Eventually, my father became the head cook.

My father had been on the farm for many years before he married and had children. I am the middle child of three.

I have an older brother named Francis and a younger sister named Emily. As children, we had many privileges that most African children did not have. We did not grow up in the villages or have to work hard to buy clothes. Although wages were not high, we were still better off than most of the Africans in an agricultural nation. My father earned more as the head cook than most teachers earned.

Once I was walking in the White field, I met the master of the land walking seven of his dogs. I was told to go around and not walk on the land. I did not want to do so and refused. She took the matter to Karanja (my father), describing the incident to him. He became angry and denied that the boy whom she was speaking of was his son. I eventually understood that there were some places that were off-limits.

We were not supposed to build permanent living quarters on our land. But my father built a two-bedroom house. Due to the potential noise and disturbance, the family eventually had to live in the village.

In 1958, my father purchased a vehicle. He was the first person of color to buy a truck. He used the truck for his businesses. At one time, he owned his own bakery while he continued working as head cook. He was loyal and enjoyed being a cook. However, through the years, these duties caused him to lose two major businesses.

My father was not educated, but he encouraged his children to get a proper education. He also made sure we were constantly exposed to the English culture. By living on the

9

farm and befriended by the white settlers, we had opportunities to read their books and be influenced by their culture. For example, many people at that time dressed in sheep skins or a piece of cloth. My father and mother dressed like Europeans.

Elizabeth II, the Queen of England, visited Kenya one day. At the time she was the Princess of Wales because her father, King George, was still alive. During her visit, she stopped at the Huxley farm. When she passed by us, she patted our heads. I noticed how beautiful she looked. A special place had been prepared for them to sit. I peeked in and saw the elaborate party and all the white farmers as they visited.

•••••

In Kenya, education is compulsory. All children go through the primary grades, called standards. When they finish standard eight, a test is given called the Kenyan Pupils' Examination (KPE). If they pass, they are admitted to Form I (high school). I entered Form 1 in 1969.

This was still fairly irregular in those days for me to enter Form I at age 13. Because of the influence of Elspeth Huxley and her mother, however, I started at age seven. They spoke to my father several times and persuaded him to send me to school early. During that time (and it has now changed), most children did not start school until they were at least ten. It was not unusual for a child of fourteen to enter Standard I.

My biggest problem in starting school at age seven was that I was always the smallest boy in the classroom. Even when I reached secondary school, the other boys were larger. They intimidated me, and often threatened to beat me if I didn't do what they wanted. As I learned later, boys tend to be the same no matter what part of the world they come from.

I eventually learned to use tricks to make sure they did not beat me up. When I was quite small, I'd provide matches or spend my pocket money to buy them cigarettes. I particularly remember sweets. That's a general term Africans used for candy, especially chocolate. Of course, such things were expensive to buy.

Since my father was the cook at the farm, sweets were not that special to us; we could have them almost any time we wanted them. He made desserts or other sweet-tasting things for his employers every day. He was not allowed to make them for himself, but he made sure, without his employers knowing, that we tasted the white man's food. I used some of my father's sweets to bribe the school bullies.

Many times, small amounts of those sweets saved me from beatings. At first I gave them to larger boys so they would not beat me up. Then I realized there were many larger boys. I finally figured out how to handle the situation.

"I'll give you some of the sweets," I said to two of the largest boys. "Each day I will bring you something. If I bring them to you, you must protect me from the other boys."

11

Their bright eyes and wide grins made it clear that I had done a wise thing. No one ever threatened me again in school; I was protected.

As I grew older, I learned to talk my way out of situations—something that would help me later in life when I faced hardships, prejudices, and adult bullying.

•••••

I don't know when I became a Christian. I don't remember ever not believing in Jesus Christ or not going to church. My parents were members of the African Inland Church and I grew up knowing the hymns and the Bible stories.

In my case, I can't speak of a specific conversion experience as some do. I can only say that Jesus Christ has always been part of my life—thanks to my godly parents. No matter how bad things became in my life—and there were some very bad times—I have never doubted God's love for me.

My trust in God would be the one thing that sustained me during my first years in America.

2
After Secondary School

When I graduated from secondary school in 1972, I had to decide what to do with my life. My father was getting older and would not be able to support me much longer.

The Kenyan education system differs from the American educational system. In Kenya there are two levels, Level 0 and Level A. The Level 0 is ordinary and we receive a diploma. Level A means you will have two more years of high school (Form V and VI). If you pass the Level A you can go to a university.

After I completed Form IV, I sat for Level 0 exams. After I passed my levels, I did not go on to the university for a two year degree. I really wanted to go to the University, but my father did not have the money to send me. So, I applied to the Bata Company.

The Bata Company operated one of the largest private shoe industries in Kenya. They had started out making cheap shoes and gradually added better-quality ones. They soon sold their products widely across Africa and in parts of Asia.

Bata had a program for management entry level for secondary school graduates. I suppose it is comparable to what we know in America as a technical school on the post high school level. I applied for admission into their management training program and was accepted. I became the first Kenyan in the program.

The training center for Bata was in Limuru, a small town just a few miles from Nairobi. Had I enrolled in the university, I would have had to move to Nairobi (about a hundred miles away) to attend Nairobi or Kenyatta Universities or travel to Makerere in Kampala, Uganda. In 1972, these were the only universities we had in East Africa.

That means the only college work I did was for Bata. They brought in instructors from Canada and other countries. It was really a business course and very much like job training so we could work for Bata after we finished the two-year course.

I completed two years of training. Before I could start the third year with Bata Shoes Company, I received a message from my father. "Benson, I want you to come home," he said.

There was no question. I did as he said. My father called me, and as a good Kikuyu son, I could not refuse. But, I was sad because I enjoyed the work and meeting people from all over the world.

My father was always an entrepreneur, "It is time for you to support yourself," he said. "You can do better if you work for yourself."

This was a major decision. I could be a manager at a growing shoe company or a business owner that touched lives of people. I knew that working for the shoe company I could see immediate benefits personally. Yet being a business owner I could influence my community and touch lives.

We started a company called "Mbayaka" ["Mbari ya Karanja" which means Karanja's Family Company]. Our company became a farming company to help small-scale farmers.

I remembered that Jesus used farming analogies many times as He taught the disciples and the people. Farming taught me patience. Seeds that are planted need time to be nurtured to produce excellent fruit. Just before I came to the United States, we planted orange trees. Over ten years later, they are flourishing. Waiting for the harvest takes patience, but it is worth the wait.

Karanja's Family Company understood that the Masai people are nomadic and travel across the Serengeti Plains with their cows, always searching for fresh grasslands. They owned the land but they never planted crops.

I went into Masai country and spoke with the tribal elders and leased land for farms from them. Once we leased the land, we planted wheat and barley. Although barley is a good grain and the people eat it, we sold most of that grain crop to breweries.

That business went very well. Initially, I handled the more administrative aspect of the business. I did not farm the land. However, that was not challenging enough to me. After two years, I bought some farm machinery and leased them to small-scale farmers. Sometimes I used the farm machinery such as the tractors and performed the work for them. They paid me.

Of course everything depended on the crops. If we had a good year, the farmers had money. If we had a bad year with drought or excessive rains, they had crop failure. This resulted in no payment for me or the Agricultural Bank.

Although some of them didn't have money, I helped them anyway. After we sold the crops, they were able to pay what they owed. I tried to make the arrangements as easy as possible for the farmers.

In the years they could not pay, I did not try to force them. If they could not pay, they could not pay. That was obvious. Sometimes it made things difficult for me, but I always agreed to wait for the next crop. I am truly glad that we did not have crop failures two years in a row and all the farmers were eventually able to pay me what they owed.

Life was difficult for most of those farmers. They were people I had lived among and cared about most of my life. In Africa, the sense of community is much stronger than in the western world. People in our communities were as close to us as our own families. The idea works like this: If we would help our immediate relatives, wouldn't we also help those who lived among us?

That kind of reasoning is simple to me because that is how I lived and was taught—my father and his father before him. It was a shock to me to experience the extreme individualism in the United States.

Drought is common in East Africa. If not drought, we have the other extreme flooding, if there is too much rain. If the crops failed, the small farmers had no where to get money. They had no insurance. Because I threw in my lot with them, when they lost money, so did I. Such situations occurred several times.

"What else could I do?" That's not perhaps the best business reply, but it is the best human response. The agreement was that I would help them with machinery so they could grow their crops. They would pay me after they sold their grain. When they did not have enough cash crops to sell, what should I have done? I believe I did the right thing; I waited.

Although I had moments of anxiety, wondering how I would pay my own bills, at the same time I had an inner peace. If I did the right thing for others, God would do the right thing for me.

I learned to wait for the next crop when we had a bad one. Just that ability to sit through the hard times was invaluable. Much later I would discover that God was at work in my life. Already the preparation had begun to teach me invaluable lessons that I would use in America.

Those situations developed a lot of patience in me. Being in the farming business does not produce quick money. We wait and we wait. With no other choice except to be patient.

Sometimes I had to borrow money from the Kenya Farmers Association (KFA) to pay my own bills. The KFA saved many of us. Through that organization, we (contractors) were able to get gasoline, diesel, fertilizer, and other products on credit.

Yes, waiting for wheat harvest or until farmers sell their corn wasn't always easy for me, especially the first time we had drought. I fretted and wondered if I could make my own payments. But God's grace was there and I was able to relax and say, "God will take care of me."

I also learned to trust God. Sometimes it was trust that God would bring the needed rain. Sometimes I had to believe that God would stop the floods or the pestilence that tried to destroy the barley. I prayed and trusted God that everyone would produce good fruit. "If they don't do well this year, next year God will make it better. There is always another year."

Those twelve years were excellent training for me. I learned to do what I could and leave the rest to God.

I often thought of Jesus' words. He spoke to the people who lived off the land. His stories were about farmers and shepherds. I remember thinking, the crops don't love the farmer; sheep can't appreciate all the time and effort the shepherds give them. Those people have to be with the animals during winter blasts or boiling summers. But they did what they needed to do—and Jesus understood that.

Many times I've told leaders and prospective leaders, "Think about farming because it is the most incredible thing that anyone can do." It is unfortunate, but many leaders today can't understand Jesus' analogies, because they have no idea what farmers must go through. They work and they wait. Sometimes their work ends in failure. But they do not give up. They can not give up. It is the only livelihood they own. They plan for the next year. And if the next year fails, they keep holding on and plant with expectations that conditions will change.

Many have never experienced such farming situations. Most of our leaders have come out of an urban, technological world. For them the farm is at the grocery store. They can not grasp how much effort and patience has to go into bringing those crops to the supermarket.

In 1981, I was privileged to visit Israel as a representative of the Kenya Farmers Association (KFA) and spent nearly three months there. KFA was an association started by the European settlers to market their crops and to borrow farming equipment, fertilizer, seed, diesel and other farming necessities. It was one of the most prestigious organizations for farmers. Farmers could open credit accounts which helped them as they waited for the harvest.

We wanted to study how Israel had redeemed the land. They became a nation again in 1948 and started with desert. How could they turn that desolate place around? If they were going to survive, they had to learn to produce crops and sell to the rest of the world. They were already doing that—and doing it quite well—when I visited. Their fruit and grain from the once-desert land now go all over the world.

Although I learned many things from the Israelis, I returned to my country with three invaluable insights. First, I discovered they have relentless determination. This helped me through my darkest days in America. They never gave up. When they faced opposition or it looked as if they might be wiped out, they persisted. "We will never give up," they said to us many times.

Israeli leaders took us many places. I heard them say that since they had become a nation, they would never again allow anybody to destroy Israel. We will defend ourselves to the last man.

I could see that determination in the way they lived. It was in their voices, even in their eyes when they spoke.

Second, they love each other. They may have had differences among themselves—like any family—but when anyone opposed them, they united and the oppressors became the common enemy.

Lastly, they are committed to their race. During the weeks I lived among them and watched them, I realized that, for them, anyone who is a Jew is important, no matter where that person lives. Even if they live in America or Europe, they are Jews and that unites them with their own.

While in Israel, I stayed at a kibbutz—a communally-owned farm. The one I visited had been settled by Jews who had immigrated from Eastern Europe. I heard about their working together, and while there, I saw their cooperation in action. Immediately, I realized that it didn't matter who they were in Europe. In Israel each person is equal.

Understanding the importance of farming, I really was eager to learn how the Israelis had been able to change a desert to become a fertile land once again. They explained how they had transported top soil from different places and poured good, rich soil over the sand. They brought in irrigation and the land changed from barren, wasteland to beautiful fertile soil where crops grow in abundance.

As I listened to them explain their history, I marveled. In many churches, people sing, jump, shout hallelujah, and cry out, "God makes a way where there is no way!" I saw first hand just how God had worked this miracle in their lives.

Since my trip in 1981, I have thought of those words differently. Isn't it better to say "God will show us how to make a way when there is no way?" We cannot sit and wait for God to do everything for us. We must work and do what we can and then God makes the way.

Indeed, all the things we need, God has already provided. Our job is to discover the answer as He guides and directs.

The Israeli people could have sought fertile land somewhere else. But, they believed God promised them the land

and that it would blossom and be fruitful. They believed God could make the desert bloom and would help them find a way to make that happen. They did what they could and God made the miracle take place.

Therefore, as a leader, I so believe. I believe that even what I am doing right now—or at any time in my life—God has given me the needed resources. They are there, but I must find them and use them. I have to figure out how to utilize those resources. God is within me and He is working with me. But God is not going to do things for me that I can do for myself.

Marriage

A fter my time of study at Bata, I set up my own business and worked closely with farmers in the area around Nakuru. My brother, Francis, had gone to college and after graduation he became a teacher and then the headmaster (principal) of a primary school about thirty-five miles from our home.

When I drove to Masai country, I had to pass by his school so I often stopped to see him. Over a period of time I got to know other members of the faculty.

One time in 1977, when I was twenty-three years old, I visited the school. "I am sorry but Mr. Karanja is not here," said one of the teachers. "You are welcome to stay and wait for him."

While I hesitated, she said, "I am Esther Wambui. Please sit down. I will make you a cup of tea."

I smiled at her. She seemed very nice and quite pretty. I didn't want to wait, but in our custom, it would be rude not to drink tea when it is offered. So I waited.

"And what do you teach?" I asked to make conversation.

"English, math, and physical education," she said. As we sipped our tea, she told me she was the coach of the girls' netball. It was obvious she was athletic and was very trim. "I also run," she added. She competed in 100-meter and 200-meter races. As soon as I finished my tea, I thanked Esther and left.

The next day Francis came to the farm. He brought his wife, Mary Njeri, along with the teacher, Esther, I had met the previous day. They stayed perhaps three hours.

Several times, Esther and I stood alone and talked. As I watched her and listened to her talk, I liked her even more. When I learned she was not married, my interest really increased.

After that, when I visited the school to see Francis, I always made sure I stopped to see Esther as well. She was a year younger than I was and had completed her teachers training college work.

It was not long before we began to date. We went to the movies or I would pick her up and travel to the Masai Land as I supervised my workers.

Esther was a Christian and a member of the Presbyterian Church of Kenya. She became a Christian at an early age. Her parents were Christians and lived in the Kikuyu land.

24

Over a period of weeks, I realized I loved her. And once I knew I loved her, I told my father to talk to her parents according to Kikuyu customs. In our culture, once a man identifies the woman he would like to marry, his family learns about her family. They consider her family background and ask many questions. Are they spiritual? Are they abusive? Are they respected? Are they people of character? Are they moral? His family also gives consideration to her family's divorce rate. If everything is favorable, they proceed with negotiations.

Once my family learned all they could about Esther's family and determined that the marriage would be acceptable, our fathers began the negotiations. We could have no wedding until the dowry was negotiated and completed. In Kikuyu culture, the dowry completes the long process. Things are gradually changing and western influence is evident. When a young man wants to marry a girl, he tells his father who then goes to the parents of the girl. The parents of the girl will ask for money. In the old days, it usually meant cattle, such as ten cows and two goats or something like that. From the western mind, it looks like buying your wife or selling your daughter. However, the Kikuyu's viewed it as an appreciation to the parents of your wife—for taking care of her.

Esther's parents wanted us to marry and they were also Christians. But they still upheld the African custom and asked for a dowry. Because things had changed, they did not want goats and other stuff. So we converted all this to cash and agreed to pay.

We married in 1977. We have three children. The oldest is Robinson Karanja, named after my father. He was born in 1978. Our second child, Juliet (to be called Julie) was born in 1979, followed in 1981 by our third child, Peter.

Destiny '87

A man named Elward Ellis came to Kenya to recruit national leaders to attend a conference in Atlanta, Georgia. They called it Destiny '87. He and Crawford Loritts, Jr. actually co-chaired Destiny '87, which was sponsored by Campus Crusade for Christ. Ellis and Loritts along with other African-American evangelical leaders shared a concern that traditional evangelical mission agencies did not adequately recruit or use minorities on their staffs. They insisted that minority evangelicals needed to participate in ministry not only in their own communities, but also throughout the entire world.

As an upcoming young leader in my church and a successful businessman, the Kenyan leadership had no problem in requesting me to represent Kenya. Other delegates included the Secretary General of the Presbyterian Church of East Africa, Dr. Wanjau, Bishop Kitonga, Pastor Ndungu, Director of Farming System of Kenya, Paul Maina and his wife, and the Executive Director of the Evangelical Church of Africa, Dr. Tukubo.

The invitation came to me through Elward Ellis, who visited Kenya and several African countries recruiting black leaders for the vision of Destiny '87. The vision of Destiny '87 was to bring black leaders together for spiritual growth and to discuss social economics for black people.

Destiny '87 paid for my airline ticket and hotel expenses. My home church paid for my meals and other expenses. I was excited, of course, because I had never been to the United States. Although I spoke English, some Americans had trouble understanding me because of my accent—a challenge I would deal with later. Somehow I communicated and attended the conference.

I was amazed. I met black leaders from all over the world and also from every denomination. They came from Brazil, New Zealand, Europe, and even Eastern Europe. The delegates were clergy and Christian business people. I met a few Muslims, but they came to the conference under the umbrella of Christianity. I was excited to be a part of the event.

At Destiny '87 the speakers kept reminding us that we had no idea of our value as black people in the world. One speaker said, "If we black people could bring all our wealth together into one nation, we would be the tenth wealthiest nation in the world."

After the third night of the conference, I sat in my hotel room. To my surprise, I began to think about getting further education. That was strange because I had stopped thinking about education years earlier. I had a successful business and I did not have to take courses at the university.

In fact, after I left Bata, Elspeth Huxley offered to help me complete my studies so I could earn a degree from London University. I applied, was accepted, and completed several courses by distance education. She was willing to give me whatever financial help I needed to go to London so that I could study there.

I turned down her offer. I reasoned that I did not need more education. I was doing very well. I was the CEO of my own company and the business was profitable. Why would I go back to my studies? I made a good salary. I played golf three times a week. I regularly played tennis and I was a member of the country club. Every day I rubbed shoulders with important business people and government officials. Why give all of that up just to have a degree?

By then my three children were enrolled in the best schools in Kenya. I thought I was through with education, not realizing that God was not through with my education.

That evening I found no rest. Perhaps I had been hearing so much about education during Destiny '87 that those words had actually penetrated me.

A number of colleges and universities set up tables and offered brochures and other literature. I made a list of educational institutions that interested me. I could see that there were opportunities for advancement. I looked at each opportunity and began thinking of advancing and leading. That was the key thing. The conference theme focused on leadership. We can be the tenth wealthiest nation. Considering my position as a contractor-farmer in my small world in Kenya, I asked myself if whatever money I have would help me? Would it give me the opportunity and platform to make sure what they are saying can happen? Could that give me a voice in this movement to encourage others that we can make a difference?

I kept thinking we could change the world. We could do something for ourselves. And yet, I said no to those things. Wealth and power were not what I wanted.

I sat in the quiet hotel room thousands of miles from my family. I knew what God wanted: Elspeth Huxley had been right to push me. I needed to advance my education. I needed to get more schooling so I could lead people. Many Africans—and others in third-world countries—had believed and taught they had to receive money or goods from outside. Destiny '87 made it clear to me that we need to advance ourselves and not depend on foreign help.

"We need to know where we are going," I said to myself. "But I can't tell people that unless I have done it myself. I have to show them the way."

As I stared into space, I realized what I had to do. I had to go back to school. I had to earn a degree.

When the thought first came to me, it seemed impossible. How could I do that? Why would I want to go to school when I was doing very well in my position?

The feeling would not go away. The more I prayed, the more certain I felt I needed to go to school. As I thought and prayed further, it was not just to go to college—but to go to a Bible college.

"That's a crazy idea," I said aloud. "Pastors go to Bible college. I don't want to be a pastor. That's not how I feel God is leading me. Surely this can't be right." The feeling would not leave me. I knew that I had to go back to college.

To many people, even to myself, this was a crazy idea because I was a successful businessman. How would I leave all of that and go to Bible college? I pondered and kept asking, "God, how can this be?"

As I sat in the hotel room and prayed, I remembered something that happened when I was about twenty years old.

One day I walked from the farm where we lived. I had traveled most of the way by truck. We reached a place where no motorized vehicle could get through, so I went on foot.

After I had been on the wandering path perhaps ten minutes, I met a Presbyterian elder whom I knew very well and he knew I was a farmer and a businessman. We greeted each other.

"Karanja! Where are you going?"

I told him.

"Do you know what? I look at you and I have one thing to tell you. You will be the greatest pastor in your church.

You will help your church."

"Thank you, mzee (a term of respect for an older man)." I started to explain that he was wrong, but he repeated his words.

"This will be so," he said.

I thought this old man spoke words of nonsense. Those words meant nothing to me.

My father had never been a pastor, and nobody in my family was a pastor. In Africa, we tended to follow the occupation of our father or other relatives. I was an active member of our church. At the time, I had no official position. Only years later would I be appointed to become part of the District Church Council.

At age twenty, I was young, unmarried, and believed he was totally wrong. In 1987, I remembered those words and could not get them out of my mind.

That's when I knew I just had to go back to college. Not just to college, but to a *Bible* college. And be what? I did not know what I wanted to be. I thought about that for a long time. I was not seriously committed, but I told God I would go wherever He led me.

The next day I walked by the booths of various colleges from around the country. I picked up several brochures and additional information. Someone introduced me to Dr. James Keiller, the Dean of Beulah Heights Bible College in Atlanta, Georgia.

We talked several minutes. It was casual because I still was not serious.

"Here, take this with you," he said and handed me a catalog and an application.

"Thank you," I replied and put the catalog away. I had no intention of opening it again.

I returned to my life in Kenya. Business was going well—in fact, better than ever. One afternoon as I walked across the farmland, I climbed a small hill that overlooked where my crops would soon flourish. I smiled. "This will be a good year," I thought. "We will have a very good year."

Something happened to me—just then. I did not hear a voice, but I knew I would not be there to harvest the crops. I would be gone.

Not only would I be gone, I would be in college—a Bible college.

"That is impossible," I said. "I don't belong in a Bible college."

I knew what was going on. My heart wanted to say yes, but my head resisted the urge.

Leaving Kenya

A fter Destiny '87, I returned to Kenya. I said nothing to my wife or to anyone else about the thoughts I had been having. I could not believe God had really spoken to me and told me to leave everything and go to college—a Bible college—in America. Or more truthfully, I did not want to believe that God was directing me to study.

I returned in July and for at least two months I said nothing about continuing my education. But the feeling about going to school would not go away. It just increased. One day I said, "God, I cannot fight this any longer. I will do as you want."

I finally told my wife.

"This cannot be," she said. "Why would God talk to you that way? How will you support the family as a student?" Esther is a very loving woman who cares for her family.

She has always been the backbone of our family. We married when we were young. We matured together. God was blessing our business and now I was ready to make a drastic change. This was very difficult for her to understand or accept. She had no excitement for America. Life was going well.

I felt so strongly about this. Yet, I had difficulty explaining the issue because of its complexity. It was a spiritual matter. I knew business and entrepreneurship—not ministry.

I spoke to friends and to our pastor. No one understood. They said I was either wrong or confused. Many said, "I don't understand how this can be."

They argued with me. "You have a good position and you are making money. You have a good home in Nakuru. Why would you choose to leave all that?"

"It doesn't sound normal to me," one of my friends said. Others could not believe that after three days at a conference I would want to give up such a nice life.

"Are you not happy?" became a common question to me.

"Why do you want to go? Why do you want to go to a Bible college?" Esther would suddenly ask. "Why would you stop what you are doing and go to the United States?"

"You have three young children, ages seven to four. And now you want to go and start a new life and become a student? How are you going to provide for me and for them? This company is doing well and you are making money. How are you going to respond to a whole company with all these people who have been depending on you and now you go?"

Several times I tried to explain to Esther, but nothing I said made sense? My only answer each time was, "This is what God wants me to do."

She would shake her head. "I do not think so," and that would end the discussion.

I prayed often and long. How could this be? I did not understand how God could speak to me and yet the people I loved most could not hear what God was saying? I prayed, "God, if I am wrong, show me; if they are wrong, show them. But please don't let this continue."

I spoke with my mother about my thoughts. "If that is what the Lord is calling you to do, go," she said. My mom was a Christian. She told me about a man that came to visit in the 1940s. She did not know his name. He looked at her hands and told her that she would have three children. One would go away with his family. That child will be the one to save the family and others. She did not believe what he said. But she saw the fulfillment.

Esther eventually stopped arguing with me over the issue. Perhaps she did not think it would do any good or maybe she saw that I was too determined.

I sent my application to three Bible colleges. One was Carver Institute in Tuscaloosa, Alabama. The second one was Philadelphia School of the Bible. The third one was Beulah Heights Bible College in Atlanta, Georgia. All of them wrote back with an acceptance. As I sorted through their responses, I felt Beulah Heights Bible College was where God wanted me to enroll. I did not know why and I could not explain it to myself. I only sensed that I was to go there.

Now I had to make my choice and it was no longer a question for me.

With the acceptance from Beulah Heights Bible College came the I-20 form. That form was the document I had to take to the American Embassy in Nairobi for them to sign so that I could apply for a student visa.

I showed Esther the I-20 and said, "Is this not proof that God wants me to go to America?"

"This is not proof," she said. "I cannot believe you want to leave here and give up everything."

"You don't want to go with me?"

"No, I do not want to go with you to America."

I had made up my mind that I was going to Bible college. Because I believed it was the will of God, I determined that nothing would stop me. I was also extremely sad because it meant I would have to go alone.

I finally told my three children, "I feel God wants me to go to the United States to study. Would you like to go with me?"

"Yes!" Robinson exclaimed.

"Me too," said Juliet. Her brother, Peter, also said he wanted to go as well.

I had no idea my children would be so excited. "We're

going to America," they rushed out to tell their friends. "We'll go to America with Daddy and then Momma will come too."

I love my kids very much and I have never been away from them. But I did not really know what I was talking about. There was no way I could have handled my kids by myself and go to school.

Esther listened to the children and their unstoppable enthusiasm.

"Okay, I'll go with you," she finally agreed. I think she wanted to hold the family together.

That whole issue had been difficult for Esther. I had provided a good home and a fine income. The people who knew us respected us. She could not understand how I would give all of that up to go to Bible college. She knew I did not want to be a pastor. Repeatedly she asked, "Why? Why would God tell you to do such a thing?"

Esther had not been the only opposing voice. Most of our friends continued to say the same things—even after they knew we were going to go.

"What are you running away from?" one friend asked.

"Have you lost your mind?" asked a relative.

I did not argue with anyone. I did not know what to do except say, "This is what God wants me to do."

I sold many of our possessions and most of the farm machinery. The rest I left with Francis to manage. The only thing I did not sell was the farm—and it still belongs to our family.

We were ready to make the move. I had my I-20 card. I had only one more step before buying the ticket: I had to get a student visa.

"Don't you know it is difficult to get such a visa," a friend asked. "And now you want all five of you to go? Why would they give you a visa?"

"If God wants me to go to America, I will come back from Nairobi with five visas," I told him.

The words may have sounded like brave bravado, but I believed what I said. I was in God's hands.

•••••

I drove to Nairobi alone and completed all the paperwork. I did not know it, but I was supposed to have taken my wife and children with me when I applied.

After completing the papers, I joined the long line. Most of the people in front of me were turned away. I saw a few of them leave with a visa stamp in their passports.

After perhaps fifteen minutes of waiting, it was my turn. I told the consulate, "I am a businessman. I want to take my wife and three children and study in the United States."

He asked me a few questions, such as "How long do you expect to be?"

"Four years," I replied. I had already figured it out. I explained that I would go all year and complete my undergraduate degree in two and a half years and then stay another eighteen months to earn a master's degree. "After that, I plan to return to work here in Kenya."

He asked two or three more questions and he stamped all our passports. That was it.

I was out of the building in less than twenty minutes. I was happy, but I had no idea how unusual it was for such a thing to happen. I can only say that the consulate must have trusted me. From there, I received my visas with no problems.

Soon we were ready to leave.

"The worst of it is now over," I said to Esther. "We shall go to Atlanta, Georgia and study. Then we shall return."

I thought life would be simple from that moment on. I did not know how wrong I was. I thought I had gone for one kind of education, but I received quite a different kind.

Welcome to Our
New Home

W hen I came to live and study in the United States, I did not know what to expect. I had already talked with Dr. Keiller, the Vice President and Academic Dean of Beulah Heights Bible College. The people at the school knew we were a family of five and would need housing. Dr. Keiller had given my information to the person in charge of housing. They had promised me a furnished apartment for five.

Dr. Francis Githieya, a doctorate student at Emory at the time, and a Presbyterian minister picked us up at the airport.

We arrived on campus at 7:30 P.M. The college was closed for Thanksgiving holiday. The manager lived on campus and was expecting us. He pointed to an old, dilapidated building across the street. "It's 899 Berne Street," he said and handed me the key. "We've been trying to fix the place up, but we are not finished."

I thanked him and we crossed the street. When I opened the door and we all stepped inside, we stared at our apartment. This was America—where we assumed everything was better than we had known in Africa.

It was not.

They had done very little to fix up the place. You could smell the fresh paint that was less than three hours old. We had two bedrooms, a kitchen, and a bathroom. You pass through the kitchen and children's room to go to the bathroom. Our bedroom served as the living room. The apartment contained two beds for five people, no bed sheets or towels, one old sofa seat, and a glass table with four chairs in the kitchen.

"This? Is this where we shall live? One room for all of us?" Esther asked. She began to cry.

"It will be all right," I said.

Of course I was disappointed. I had not expected a place as nice as our home in Nakuru, but I had expected an apartment to accommodate the five of us. I did not think that there would be anything like this in the United States.

"Where are our bedrooms?" asked Robinson.

I shook my head, "This is where we shall live. All of us, right here."

"In one room?" asked Juliet. "Only one room?"

It was a most devastating thing. The fresh paint smell was very strong. It was cold. I could not get the small heater on the wall to work. I had to ask for help. We made the adjustment. Dr. Glthieya and his wife, Marie, loaned us some linens and utensils. After we bought our own from the thrift store, we returned theirs to them. They took us to Simpson's Grocery Store to buy food. If it were not for Francis and his family, it would have been very difficult.

Dr. Richard Edwards brought us some Kentucky Fried Chicken. His wife, Connie, assisted us in getting our children enrolled in school. Connie would pick up the children for school and bring them home. We will be forever grateful for their assistance with the children.

For nine months all five of us lived in that one room. People visited me and we invited them to sit. We had a sofa, four chairs, and our bed. The boys share the bed and Juliet slept on the sofa before we bought a twin bed from the thrift store. That was all the furniture. So when more than one person came to visit, someone had to sit on our bed.

Today, I smile about the room where the five of us lived. It brings an even bigger smile to me when students come to the college and we assign them one-room apartments. They rush back to the office, "It is too small," they complain.

I don't argue. "That is all we have," is my answer. I rarely tell them about what we went through.

The apartment that Beulah Heights Bible College was supposed to fix up never got fixed. Only later as I learned how things worked, did I realize that the office manager could easily have seen that our place was repaired or at least improved. I don't know why he never had any work done, unless, it was to save money. The school was quite poor in those days.

The worst part of the nine months is the humiliation my wife faced. "This is what you have brought us to America to live in?"

I understood her hurt and her anger. Had I not been fully convinced that God wanted me to study at Beulah Heights Bible College, I would have left after the first day. But I knew I was exactly where God wanted me to be. I had peace; but my heart ached for my wife and my three children.

In Africa, each child had a bedroom. We owned three cars and our kids never had to walk to school. Now, we had no car and one bedroom.

I was 35 years old. It was sad to realize that I had been so successful in my home country and now I was coming to this.

I had no idea that the situation would grow worse.

But, it did get worse.

I had neither a work permit nor a green card to work in the United States. It would take nine months to qualify to apply for one. Esther had no green card, so she could not work. That was not only humiliating, but she had nothing to do all day long. I sat in the classrooms, learning and mixing with others. Esther was alone. It was depressing.

However, through it all, I remained at peace. I had brought $10,000 from Kenya—which was a lot of money for that country—but I knew the money would not sustain us long.

Before I knew I needed a green card (which gives aliens the authorization to work), I went out to find a job. Not far from the college was a fast-food place called Krystals. They hired me to work on the third shift. I worked from midnight until seven the next morning. Before I went there, I knew nothing about fast-food chains. I did not know the types of food they served or the ingredients.

The worst part of my working at Krystals was that the other employees were high school students. None of the supervisors were older than 25. They were more like people I had employed when I was CEO of my own company.

It was a big adjustment. Many times I reminded myself that I was an employee and at the bottom of the list. I was older and had many life experiences. I knew some of their business methods were not good. But I said nothing. I reminded myself that I was there to work, not to correct.

The first two weeks were extremely difficult for me. The people treated me well. I have no complaints about that. But the customers who came in after midnight were sometimes drunk and at other times just lonely and wanted to sit with a cup of coffee.

The first Friday night was extremely difficult for me. My supervisor told me to work the window. That surprised me because my English was not very good and my accent made it difficult for many people to understand me.

Drivers pulled up at the window and gave me their orders. They spoke quickly—or so it seemed to me—and shouted their order. I had to run from the window into the kitchen and prepare the things they wanted.

"One hamburger with no pickle," the customer ordered.

I did not understand a single word beyond, "hamburger." I made a hamburger and put everything on it.

"I said no pickle. Didn't you hear me? No pickle!"

I apologized and rushed back into the kitchen to remove the pickles before I could serve him.

I made many mistakes. I heard many complaints and yelling. But I never said more than, "I am sorry, sir." Once I said those words, their anger seemed to evaporate.

For two and a half weeks, I worked at Krystals and I did not complain. I rarely got enough sleep—and that would become my practice for most of the next ten years. We faced hardships and loneliness. My wife was sad and missed her family and friends in Nakuru.

This may sound strange, but I knew God was at work in my life. I had no understanding why I had to go through such things, but I was always at peace.

About that time, the school had an opening in the maintenance department. I heard about it and asked if they would hire me. They did. It was a good thing because that's when I realized I should not have worked at Krystals. I did not have a green card and they could have had problems with the government.

I took the job in maintenance at the college. One of my jobs was to finish working on my apartment. Although that apartment was supposed to have been ready for me when I moved in, it was not finished. During the time I was on the maintenance crew (the next two and a half years), it never did get completed. They eventually tore the building down.

Life was not always so bad. There were many good moments. For instance, I had never seen snow. In Kenya, we have several snow-capped mountains, but I lived in an equatorial country and had only read about the snow.

During the winter of 1987, Atlanta had the largest snow-storm many of the residents had ever seen. When the area did get snow, it is usually only an inch or two. That year, it was very deep. The drifts and piles around the buildings were nearly three feet high.

After our son saw the snow, he dressed and raced out of the building. Robin tried to walk on the snow, but his feet slid and he fell backward. He got up and tried again. The second time, he fell forward, hit his chin on the ice underneath. He badly cut his lip.

He ran into our apartment screaming, and we saw the blood streaming down his chin.

What was I to do? I did not have insurance. I did not know what to do or where to take him. School was not in session and no one was around to ask to drive him to a doctor or to the emergency room.

Esther washed off his lip and I saw a large cut. Not knowing what else to do, I got dressed and walked about 4 miles to the Kroger store and bought bandages. With needle and thread, I stitched his lip together. His mouth healed, but even today, he carries a small scar.

• • • • •

I had to work. At the school, they paid me by providing our housing and my tuition. I did not know how to do many of the jobs. But I gave my best to anything I saw that needed doing. On the snow day, the people on salary did not have to come to work and they would still get paid. If I did not work, I would not get paid, so I had to show up.

As soon as the snow stopped, I went into the office. The Office Manager was there; he lived on the property. I asked him what I should do.

"No one is doing anything with maintenance," he said. "Go home today."

"Yes, I can do that." I said. "But if I do, there is no money for me. Please, if there is any work I can do, please allow me to do it."

He thought for a few minutes before he said, "Okay, go all around the campus and collect the trash."

I knew where they stored the wheelbarrow. I took it and went to all the classrooms, offices, and dorms. I collected all the trash and garbage. I was extremely cold—the coldest I had ever been in my life. I had no heavy coat, but I did have a pair of gloves. The wind blew so much that the gloves did little to protect me.

I worked all morning, and at noon I went back to our apartment for lunch. When I opened the door, Esther and the children were hunched together on the bed. They were all crying.

"What is wrong?" I asked. "Who is sick?"

Esther finally stopped crying and said, "Why did you do this to yourself—to us? Why did you have to bring us to this—this torture?"

"What is wrong?" I grabbed my wife and children and hugged them.

"We saw you out there," Esther said. "We saw what you were doing. Why do you have to push that wheelbarrow and pick up everyone's garbage? How can you sink so low?"

They had watched me push the wheelbarrow through the drifts as I went from building to building.

For a few seconds I said nothing. When bad weather came in Kenya such as heavy rain, we never let our employees work under such conditions.

"What kind of a country is this?" she asked. She took my frozen hands in hers and fresh tears flowed.

I don't remember what I said to her. But I tried to help her calm down. "It will not always be this way," I said. "I know this is a bridge to something that is greater than what I am doing right now."

Esther was disappointed and discouraged, but I truly was all right. "If I allow this condition to upset me," I said, "it will distract me and I will never arrive where God wishes to take me."

I spoke to my family for several more minutes before they were calm. We prayed together and I think they felt a little better.

Even on that cold, snow-filled day, I had a sense of where I was going. I already had my goals and I would not allow anything to stop me. I would finish Beulah Heights Bible College, go to another school, earn a master's degree, and then earn my doctorate in business. I did not plan to be away from Africa for more than ten years.

"It will be all right," I whispered. "It will be all right."

Although nothing looked that way, I knew the situation was only temporary.

• • • • •

We were in the one bedroom apartment when the American holiday, Thanksgiving, came. I did not know anything about Thanksgiving. But people talked about it, the holiday, and the food. Francis and his family invited us to their apartment.

Then Christmas came. One of the students, who also worked at the college, invited us to go to his church on Christmas Eve. He was a member of a Salvation Army church and volunteered to pick us up.

He took us to church and that night they observed Holy Communion. It surprised me that everyone around me took the bread and the juice. Esther and I stared at each other, not comprehending. I had come from the Africa Inland Church and my wife from the Presbyterian. But, not every person took Holy Communion—only the pastors and leaders felt were worthy.

Many of the churches in Africa, on such special Sundays

where they serve communion, dismiss everyone and invited those back inside who were welcomed to the Lord's Table. This was a new experience for us.

When I asked my friend, he said, "If you are a Christian and if your children are believers, they may take it. It is a matter between them and God."

All five of us took Holy Communion.

At the end of the Christmas Eve service, the pastor introduced himself. I have no idea how he knew we were not American blacks, but the first question he asked was, "Where are you from?"

He spoke to us for several minutes and made us feel truly welcome. Christmas Eve was Thursday and he asked where we lived. When we told him at Beulah Heights Bible College, he said, "On Monday I'll send somebody to come and buy your kids some clothes to wear for the winter. They need warmer clothing."

I thanked him for all of us. From the corner of my eye, I saw tears slide down Esther's cheeks.

True to his word, the pastor sent someone to our apartment. They took our children to a store and bought them warm clothes. After they returned, our kids kept running around showing off their new clothes. They ran outside in the cold and came back in, delighted that they were warm enough to play outside.

• • • • •

We stayed in the one room apartment for nine months

until Paul, the man in charge of maintenance, graduated in May of 1988. He stayed another two months before he left. When he moved on, I applied for his job and received it. That meant we were able to leave our still unrepaired, one-bedroom apartment and move into one with two bedrooms. We had become so accustomed to the tiny place, a second bedroom felt luxurious. It was a white building, and we used to talk about living in the white house.

I also received a raise in pay. Instead of $3.25 an hour, I was making $3.60. I was the janitor and maintenance person.

By then, my children had been in the United States about a year and knew how people lived. They could not understand why they had once had so much and now had almost nothing. Before I had bought my shoes at Florsheim and now I went to Payless—when I could afford a pair of shoes.

To their credit, my children did not complain. I know it was difficult for them, especially when they saw other children who had so much more than we did.

Only after they had grown up and we were able to live a comfortable middle-class lifestyle, did they talk about those days.

"Do you know how much we were humiliated by kids because of wearing those cheap shoes?" Juliet once said.

"I'm sorry, but—"

"No, we understood. You could not afford to buy anything better. We knew what we were going through."

I wept that day. My children had suffered so much, but they had never complained.

At the time we arrived in Atlanta, Robin was in middle school and children can be so cruel.

Nowadays, they tell me how they cried or how humiliated they felt because of unkindness of other kids. I've always loved my kids; now I love them even more for being so understanding.

One day Juliet said to me, "Dad you don't know what we went through."

The two-bedroom apartment was larger, but it was in terrible shape. When we finally moved out after eighteen months no one else moved in. The college tore down the building. They had to tear it down—it was falling down. The building had functioned primarily as a storage area where they put things for years.

I had a living room, but it was not unusual to see a large rat run across or to see roaches everywhere. At the time, there were few international students, a total of five of us.

I am especially grateful to an older student, Nola Love. She opened an alteration shop and would bring me clothes that people had not picked up. The best jacket I wore during my student days was one she gave me.

One time she visited our one-bedroom apartment. "Why are you staying here?" she asked. "Why can't you move and get a good apartment?"

"I cannot afford one off campus," I said.

I looked at the situation in two ways. The rent was not

free, but it was cheaper than if we moved somewhere else. I would also have to get transportation back and forth.

The school never gave me any money for my work, not one dime. Everything I earned went to pay for my tuition and my apartment. I had to pay for our clothes and food from the money I had brought with me from Africa.

I soon learned that I could take the family to a thrift store and for twenty dollars I could buy something usable for all of us.

Esther was finally able to bring in a few dollars by cleaning houses or helping in a day-care center. She did not have a green card, but the people took pity on her.

Mostly, of course, we bought food and clothes from the money I had brought with me. Each day, I realized that withdrawing without depositing could not take us far.

In time, Esther accepted that this was the leading of God's Spirit. But it was not easy and it took her a long time.

Even though she questioned, she still supported me in every way. But she did not have inner peace for a long time, perhaps until the end of our first year.

I could not have done what I did without her. I worked long hours, studied, and went to school full time. For ten years I worked for my undergraduate degree, completed two master's degrees, and my doctorate. During those years, I never worked less than fifty hours a week.

Esther was always there supporting me. My children never turned bitter. They loved me. With their help, I made it through those years.

In 1991, Robin became very sick. He ate something and had a serious allergic reaction. His nose began to swell and he hurt badly. The school called me and said I should take him to Grady Hospital. I rushed him there. Grady Hospital is in the center of Atlanta and treats indigents free or on a sliding scale. They would not even give me a discount at Grady. "Grady Hospital," the admitting clerk said, "is for citizens."

I sighed. They did help me set up a plan so I could pay each month. I handed them my credit card.

Things have changed since I had those experiences, but we still have a long way to go before we make it easy for internationals to make their way in this country. Today, for example, the college has educated students from over 30 countries and about 15 percent of the student body are international students.

When I see them struggling, I'm deeply torn. They need to pay like everyone else; but sometimes they need help and encouragement. Many times I've said to my staff, "You don't know what's going on with that student. Let's be patient and as helpful as we can."

Perhaps, I still remember too vividly my own experience. So far as I'm aware, none of my classmates knew what was going on with me. The staff at Beulah Heights Bible College did not know, or knew very little.

Elward Ellis visited us in Atlanta in January 1988, a few months after I had started school. We had come from a warm country and I had nothing heavy enough for winter in Atlanta.

When Elward saw what we wore, he said, "I want to buy you and Esther winter coats." The Salvation Army had coats for children at Christmas.

We were so grateful and thanked him. He took us to Macy's Department Store in a large shopping mall, the most expensive store in the mall. This was 1988 and he said he would pay $100 for a coat for me. That was a lot of money to us in our situation. "That is too much money," I protested.

"But, I want to give this to you," he said.

"Why don't you do this?" I asked. "Rather than spend $200 on that, give us $100. We will buy a good warm coat at K-Mart and it will be all right.

"But it will not be the same quality," he said and laughed.

"I have been in K-Mart. They have good quality—at least good enough for us for now."

"No Benson, I know the difference."

"You can spend that money," I said, "but I'd be more comfortable if you could give me the money, and I know I'll even save money from this $100." Remember he wanted to spend almost $200 to buy us quality jackets and I was saving him money by saying give us $100 and we would buy from K-Mart. I did not know the difference in the quality between K-Mart and Macy's, but I did know the difference in price.

We talked for several minutes and then he shrugged his shoulders and handed me five twenty-dollar bills.

He was a friend. He had proved it in the best way possible. He provided clothes when we needed them badly.

We had no insurance and no money to buy any. We did learn about a free clinic. Central Presbyterian Church in Atlanta had a clinic just for people like us. They saw us for free or provided treatment at the lowest possible cost to us. They also had a dentist to clean teeth. My children also received dental care.

I do not know how we would have made it through those ten years without Central Presbyterian Church. Although we were not members of the church, the clinic still cared for us. They were good Samaritans. They served without expectation of anything in return. My family and I truly appreciated their ministry to us during those challenging times. The doctors and staff could have been devoting their energies in a practice to generate a nice income, yet, they were compelled to serve and give of their time, knowledge, and resources. Central Presbyterian Church blesses the urban community they serve. Those able to experience their care have been truly touched by their kindness and generosity.

Best of Times,
Worst of Times

A t Beulah Heights, at various times they had a cafeteria. Someone would start one and it would go a few months. Then it would fail and someone else would come in and try.

During my student years, beginning in the fall of 1987, I worked for minimum wages; but because I was not a dorm student, I could not eat in the cafeteria. Only staff and dorm students were allowed to eat in the cafeteria.

Our money was draining away and we had to count every bit of food we bought. Each month, we did not know if we could make it until the next.

At that time, a gentleman who was married to a Japanese woman was in charge of the cafeteria. I never told them about our situation, but he was able to see how poor we were. One time I came inside at the end of the meal to empty the garbage.

"Have you eaten?" he asked. I shook my head no.

"Then sit,"he said. "We have plenty left." He did that almost every evening for several weeks. Many times, he wrapped food for me to take home to my family. But someone in the administration building learned what the man was doing.

"He is not eligible to eat here," the office manager said. "He is not a dorm student."

Even though the cook pointed out that there was plenty of food, the office manager said he could not feed me.

By then, my wife had started to work at a day-care center. Our reserves were almost gone, but I bought a car—a 1982 Mazda for $1,200. Beulah Heights Bible College is at least a mile from the bus line and there was not good transportation in that part of the city. Each afternoon, I drove to the day-care center on Cleveland Avenue, picked her up, and drove her home. I had a thirty-minute break to drive her home. It was usually six o'clock before we returned.

She would cook our evening meal and I came in about 6:30 P.M.

Despite what the office manager said, the cook would often call me into the cafeteria. If he had left over food, he packed it and handed it to me—all the time making sure the office manager never saw what he was doing.

He often packed greens and other vegetables that were leftover. We rarely received meat or chicken because they were usually gone.

I can never forget his kindness. He did not have to do that and I had no way to pay him. At times, I felt as if I were Elijah in the wilderness and the cook was like the ravens that fed him.

"You are like the ravens that fed Elijah," I told him once.

During those times when he gave me food, I used to think about the hyena in Kenya. The hyena does not kill his prey, but he eats what the lions or other animals kill and leave. They go to the place where the lions are feeding and walk around. As soon as the lions have been filled and move away, the hyena can go in and pick over whatever is left. But the lion can turn around and kill or let the hyena out.

As the days went by, I learned that, like the hyena, I had to figure out exactly the right time. I did not want to go near the cafeteria while anyone was eating. I could not go too late after the leftovers had been packed away.

I suppose I could have become bitter. I chose not to allow bitterness to creep in. The school paid me practically nothing for my work—the minimum wage applied to my rent and tuition. "This is God's will that I am doing," I reminded myself when life became difficult for me.

My wife's salary was slightly over one hundred dollars a week. When Esther brought home her money, we planned for the next week. This was true all through my undergraduate days at Beulah Heights. After I entered graduate school I had to make adjustments, but things were still at a minimum. We had to plan the week's groceries. We had no extra money.

Peter, our youngest, wanted a basketball, but I could never afford one. I did not want to use that kind of language, so I would say, "I'll buy you one next week."

Every week, he would ask and I would give him the same answer. Eventually, he stopped asking. In 2002, he said to me, "Dad, do you remember how many times you promised to buy me that basketball and you didn't?"

"Yes, I remember very well."

"It is all right. I can understand now. I didn't then, but I do now."

"But you never complained," I said.

It was not easy for any of us, but we did the best we could. Once Esther overcame her disappointment and was able to work, she became totally supportive. She worried at times, but no longer talked of going back to Africa.

We wanted our children to have a treat at least once a week—something special—and they liked pizza. So every Friday, we bought pizza at the grocery store because it was the cheapest treat we could find.

"I don't want any more pizza," Juliet said on Friday. "I want Chinese."

"I know children, but we can't afford Chinese."

"Daddy, we need Chinese," Peter said.

"Please Daddy," Robin added. "I'm tired of pizza."

This time Esther was on their side, "Let's buy Chinese," she said, "this one time. We can do it."

"That will cost us twenty dollars," I said. I was always the frugal one and held on to every penny I could.

They still begged for Chinese.

"You are ready to jump me, aren't you?" I asked. "Okay, Chinese it is tonight—tonight only!"

As we ate, I watched their faces. I had no idea how we would pay all our bills, but the joy of their faces was worth the money. And of course, we paid our bills. God always made a way.

The "Karanja" family after two years of living in Atlanta, Georgia, USA.
Back row, my daughter Juliet on my right, and my wife Esther on my left
Front row, my youngest son Peter and my eldest son Robinson

Relaxing in the park, after a hard day's work.

Cutting the lawn at BHBC for the Maintenance Department. Who would have thought that I would one day be the President of Beulah Heights University.

Studying in my dorm room.

While preparing for my BA degree, I was often burning the midnight oil.

My graduation day—
Where do I go from here?

After just a few years as an employee with BHBC,
I was promoted to the Financial Aid Department.

A typical day in the office of
Beulah Heights Bible College.

My graduation day was truly a milestone that
I will always remember. I was overjoyed to receive
my Master of Business Administration
degree from Brenau University.

Role Models and Mentors

"**W**hat inspired you?"

"How could you go through such humiliation?"

I hear these questions often. I have no problem with the answer. Of course, it is my faith in a faithful God that has enabled me to go through many difficult places.

I have also had mentors. One of them was the first president of Kenya, Jomo Kenyetta. I heard his story a few years after our independence and he became my role model — and my mentor, even though we never met.

If any man had a right to be bitter, to hate white people, to stir up the nation against them, it was the people referred to as Mzee (literally, means a respected elder, a term of deep respect).

Briefly, Jomo Kenyatta was educated in Kenya but went to

Great Britian for thirteen years, beginning in 1931. When he returned to Kenya, he began to work for independence—an unheard thing in Africa. (In 1958, Gold Coast, later known as Ghana, was the first African country to receive their independence.) He was a leader ahead of his time. The British arrested him in 1952 and he was either imprisoned or under house arrest until independence in 1963. He formed a political party, won the first election, and remained president until his death in 1978.

Like Mandela of South Africa, Kenyatta is remembered as a brave and charismatic leader who suffered imprisonment in his bid for political independence for his country. During all the years he remained in England, he worked at odd jobs, and nothing was beneath him. He was treated badly by many people in England, but he was never bitter. After his arrest and during his imprisonment, Mzee Kenyatta encouraged people to work for independence without violence, not to fight the British.

When Kenyatta returned to Kenya in 1952, he mobilized the Africans to strive for independence. For 17 and a-half years he lived with the missionaries in Europe and England. He suffered and never held a good job. But when he came back to Kenya he started mobilizing Africans to ask for independence.

And through the process, in 1952, he was jailed for seven years. He was sentenced to life in prison and then it was reduced to, I believe, seven and a half years. He was imprisoned at Malal, which is on the border of Sudan and Kenya.

It was a deserted and forlorn place. He could not escape. If he had escaped in those days, there was nothing but desert and wild animals. Soldiers would have caught him or the animals would have killed him. They released him from house detention in 1962.

I still remember his speech when he came out of his house arrest. A reporter asked, "Mzee Kenyatta, are you bitter?"

"No, I am not bitter, but I have learned something. All those years I was in the university to learn that we have to work hard and be faithful to make our independence mean all that we want and hope. If we do nothing and get bitter, there will be many difficulties and nothing will be achieved." He also wrote a book about suffering without bitterness.

We all can learn a lesson about bitterness from Mzee Kenyatta—to suffer without getting bitter. And even if we get bitter when we go through trying times, we should just push forward and use these experiences to help with the next one. And remember that whatever place we find ourselves in is temporary and that tomorrow will be another day.

They also asked him what political party he would join. He said, "I don't know. I've been out of circulation for a long time and for now I'm going to position myself and try to understand what is going on and then I will know. First, I want to put my life together."

Shortly after that, the Mzee visited Nakuru to address the white settlers. This is not verbatim, but it is what I remember.

73

"I'm not angry at you." He repeated that sentence several times and he added, "But from now on, I don't want to come to you as a master or a servant. You are good Kenyans, as I am. You may even know better than I do what we want for this country. We want to work together here in our country, Kenya, for the education of our children. If our Kenya is to progress, our children must have good schools." He finished his speech with an African word *harambee* (meaning working together or teamwork).

The word means to pull together or to unite. Harambee became the unifying word about Kenyans for the next few years. Everywhere people went, they heard the cry, "Harambee!"

Modern leaders emphasize teamwork, but Kenyatta knew from the beginning that the people had to pull together. Kenya was a poor country and he told them that nothing would happen unless they unite and support each other.

After independence, Kenya had two political parties. The Mzee joined Kenya African National Union (KANU) as a member; the opposition party was called Kenya African Democratic Union (KADU). When the elections came, KANU easily won at the polls. In his victory speech, Kenyatta said something like this:

"Listen to me. When you go home and say we KANU have won or we KADU have lost, you are an enemy of Africa and the people of Kenya. You are an enemy of African freedom. The victory today is for all Kenyans KANU or KADU, black, white, Arabs, and Indians. I want you to know that the biggest achievement we have received today is an achievement for all peace-loving people, white, brown, or yellow. They are all Kenyans."

Our first president inspired me. I hope readers can understand why. During my darkest and most lonely days at Beulah Heights Bible College, I reminded myself that the Mzee had been treated worse than I ever would be, and he did not grow bitter.

When I was sweating and cleaning in the summer, or cutting the grass, I said to myself, "I'm not going to be bitter because nobody put me here. I'm here because I want to do something. So, I can't be angry. This is the path I must take to reach my goals. I can't look back and say this is what I was. If I want to go somewhere then I've got to go through this. I've got to be refined. I've got to prepare myself, and there is no other way to prepare myself than what I'm going through."

Such determination gave me peace.

In the first years I worked at the college, they paid me the legal minimum wage of $3.25 an hour. Sometimes I worked ten hours a day because I was the only janitor and the maintenance person at that time. The college had a student body of less than a hundred.

My journey through all the years at Beulah Heights Bible College taught me many things. It taught me to appreciate anything God brings me. It taught me to be patient. It taught me to love everybody. It taught me to put myself in other people's shoes. So, even today as a leader when I walk around campus and I see people cleaning, I don't see them as janitors. I see people working as a team. I know that if those bathrooms are not cleaned, I can not be a good president. If the library's books are not shelved, I can not be a successful president. If the teachers or the faculty are not teaching properly, I can not be a successful president.

Those early days at Beulah Heights Bible College prepared me to understand. Over the next fifteen years, I worked as a janitor, Librarian, and the Vice President for Student Services. It was training—a special university, a personal journey that I had to travel alone. This personal journey built a character that I could not have received from any institution. It gave me a taste of patience and humiliation and a better understanding of how God works.

9
MOVING ON

A fter I completed my undergraduate work at Beulah Heights Bible College in 1990, I applied to Emory University in Atlanta to work on my Master in Business Administration degree. When I realized the fees were so expensive, I knew I could not afford to go to school there. I applied to Brenau University in Gainesville, Georgia. Although that was also expensive, it was still less than half of what Emory charged. Brenau accepted me, so I registered. I had my Mazda, and I had to drive about an hour each way.

Since I was not a United States citizen, I could not apply for any financial aid assistance. I did not know how I would make the payments to Brenau. But, I truly believed God was speaking to me to pursue my education.

The registrar at Brenau gave me a time-payment plan. Occasionally, I received small scholarships that paid for a single class, but not many. After much prayer and agony, I applied for credit cards. Despite the high interest rates, whenever I could not afford to pay for everything at the end of the month, I charged it. The interest mounted and I groaned at the large bill I would eventually have to pay. But credit cards helped us survive those first years.

The credit cards gave me an opportunity to make payments, although the interest rates nearly choked us. I used a credit card several times to pay my tuition at the college. At no point did the office give me a break on paying late.

While I stayed at Beulah Heights, I continued to work long hours with small pay. Esther's work at the day care helped. After eighteen months in 1992, I received my master's degree in business administration.

About the time I finished my work at Brenau, I heard from a former missionary to Kenya named Jim Woolrick who lived in the Chicago area. I knew Jim and we played tennis together quite often when he served in Nakuru.

Shortly after I had arrived in Atlanta, I wrote or telephoned all of the former missionaries I had known. I knew so little about the United States and our family suffered a lot during that first year. I decided to ask them for help.

"This is Benson" I would say, "I'm now living in Atlanta."

When I explained my situation, I received responses such as, "Have you spoken to your pastor?" "Have you asked the school for help?" Often they gave me names of other people to contact. They did not have to help nor did

78

they owe me anything. But it did hurt. I presumed we had a friendship—obviously one that did not exist.

I would call some missionary friends and leave a voice message, but none of them returned my call.

Getting no response from the calls did not discourage me. In fact, it made me more resolved than ever. I had enough pride in myself and my abilities that I knew we would make it. But more importantly, God had brought us to this country; now it was up to God to provide for us. Many months, I had no idea where money would come from to pay our bills or where we would get food. But, we did not miss any meals or go without the things we truly needed.

• • • • •

Jim Woolrick was the one exception among the former missionaries I had known. He not only wanted us to visit, but he sent money for me to drive all five of us to visit him.

At that time, Jim worked for ServiceMaster—a company that specialized in anything from lawn care to termite control. The day after I arrived, Jim set up a meeting and introduced me to the chairman and CEO of ServiceMaster.

That's when I learned that ServiceMaster wanted to recruit someone to become their director of Europe, the Middle East, and parts of Africa. At that time, the summer of 1992, they had started to sell their services and products in South Africa.

I was surprised, but excited. By the time I left Chicago, I was quite sure they would offer me the position. I had several interviews while I was there. What made me most confident was that I had met the CEO, which was not a normal practice.

In the interviewing process, I told them I had finished my MBA and was open to any job.

We had a wonderful time in Chicago and Jim encouraged me greatly. We returned to Atlanta and the very next day, Dr. Samuel Chand called me.

Sam Chand was born in India and came to Beulah Heights Bible College as a student in 1973. He graduated and became a pastor in Michigan. While pastoring, he continued his education and showed outstanding leadership. In 1989, two years after I became a student, the board of trustees asked Sam to become their president. Jim Keiller stayed on as Vice President and Academic Dean.

When Sam asked me to come to his office, he explained that the college had applied for accreditation with TRACS— Transnational Association of Christian Colleges and Schools. I knew that, but his next sentence amazed me.

"I would like you to help me."

"Help you?" I asked. "How can I help you?"

"I would like you to help us in establishing the department of financial aid. Since we have received TRACS accreditation, our students can start receiving financial aid from the government."

Sam Chand is an extremely persuasive fellow and someone I liked very much.

At the time he asked, I still lived on campus (and paid

rent), worked in the library and studied at Brenau University.

Sam had no knowledge that the people at ServiceMaster had interviewed me or that I was prepared to accept an offer if they wanted to hire me.

I hesitated to say yes to Sam. I did not tell him about ServiceMaster. "Well, tell me more," I said, giving myself time to think of a response.

As I listened, a thought occurred to me. Maybe this is an opportunity for me to complete my doctorate. I had applied for entrance at Clark Atlanta University in Atlanta before I left for Chicago. At that time, I wanted to do a doctorate in international business. Rather than go to Europe or wherever ServiceMaster would send me, I could stay in Atlanta and finish my education.

"You can teach one or two classes," Sam said, "and at the same time you can become the Fiscal Officer, as well as work in the library."

"That sounds interesting," I said.

"The total package for you is $800 per month."

That was quite a jump from the $4.25 an hour I was earning. The single negative factor was that there would be no medical benefits.

I was still thinking through what Sam said and weighing the other job opportunity. Hardly conscious of what I was doing, I said, "All right."

Sam was elated.

I then learned a staggering fact: The college did not have

the money to pay me. They could not afford to pay the $800. In fact, I had to wait for three months before I got my first $800 check.

I started the Financial Aid Department at Beulah Heights Bible College and held the title of Fiscal Officer. I dealt with the finances and made sure that everything was recorded correctly, according to the federal government requirements.

They hired another person, Hayward Clark, to be the Director of Financial Aid, which made him my boss. Until I was hired in 1992, the college had never hired an African or a black man to hold any position. It was a small institution but still a very conservative one. Although they had many black students, especially in the night classes, they had no African or Black Americans who actually taught or held any position in the school. I became the first black staff member to hold an official position.

I can smile now as I think of those days. Pastor Hayward and I shared an office. Both of us had desks. He also had a nice chair and the only telephone in the room sat on his desk.

I enjoyed teaching the accounting and finance management classes at the college. I also had my job as Financial Aid Fiscal Officer. That was quite an experience for me. Although my desk did not have a phone, I was the one who needed the telephone most of the time. For several months, it was quite difficult. I constantly had to leave my desk and go to the other one. Sometimes he would be talking and I would have to stand and wait for him to finish.

Finally, they moved us into two different offices. I had a telephone on my own desk. I still did not have a decent chair. I had one of those hard, brown plastic chairs—the kind they used in the classroom. It was certainly not an office chair and not comfortable for me to sit in for hours at a time.

Several times, Dr. Chand passed by my office. One day he noticed the chair, "When are they going to get you a good chair?"

"I don't know," I said. "I'm waiting." I did not tell him that I had been waiting nearly five months.

Three more times during the next month, Dr. Chand passed my office and saw that I had not received a chair. One afternoon, Dr. Chand came by my office and noticed I was still sitting on the brown chair. "You still have no chair, do you?"

"I am waiting," is all I said.

He walked out of my office, went down the hallway into his office. He picked up his chair and brought it to me. "Here is your chair," he said. He turned and walked out.

I watched him as he went to the business manager's office. "I want another chair for my desk by this afternoon," he said and walked back to his office.

That's how I got a decent office chair. That is also one of the many reasons I deeply respect Dr. Chand. He cared. And he showed his care.

At that time, I was working part-time at Laurel Heights

Children's Hospital, a psychiatric hospital not far from Emory University. I had been working for them since 1990. I would put in 30 hours at Beulah Heights Bible College handling the financial aid affairs and volunteering in the library for $800.00 per month. Then I would also spend several hours each week at the hospital as a behavior specialist. These were interesting times of great learning and gaining experience.

Laurel Heights

I started to work at Laurel Heights Children's Hospital in 1990, shortly after I graduated from Beulah Heights Bible College. I worked on the units as a behavior specialist. That was a challenging experience for me. I worked with children between the ages of five and eighteen—from children to young adults. I learned invaluable life lessons while I was employed there.

In 1992, shortly after I had completed my MBA at Brenau, I learned there was an opening for a Director of Marketing at Laurel Heights. I applied, but I did not get the position.

Instead, they hired a woman—a woman with a powerful personality. I was highly qualified for the position, but they did not even call me for an interview. To make it even more strange, while I worked on the unit as a behavior specialist, the woman, as the new Director of Marketing, asked me to write a business document for Laurel Heights.

I did it and was glad to do so. They did not pay me a dime for the extra hours. But, they used my work. Was I bitter? Yes, I was at first. It took me time and much prayer to move beyond that. They had not given me the courtesy of an interview, but they did not mind using my expertise— without payment.

Although I had known, I learned in the most practical way possible that life is not always fair. People will take advantage of us. I also realized that God would provide better opportunities for me if I refused to hold any grudges or resentment. I wanted to be ready to take the next steps when the doors of opportunity opened for me.

For two and a half years, I worked at Laurel Heights. It became obvious they were never going to consider me for anything more. It was also obvious I could not continue working two jobs. When Sam offered me the full-time position, I knew it was time to take advantage of the opportunity to work at one job full-time.

But again, that was another journey of rejection. Did I respect that woman who had gotten the job for which I was better qualified? Sure I did. When I left, I met with her and it was a sad parting. I liked her and she genuinely liked me. Despite her liking me, I do not think she ever saw me as anything more than a black person.

I had worked in the unit and I was second from the bottom because there were janitors below me. In the pecking order, there were janitors, then the behavior specialists; above us were nurses, office staff, and doctors. The supervisors were at the top.

The doctors never treated me as one step above the janitors. Most of them respected my opinion. They often chatted with me, and many of them would invite me to eat in the cafeteria with them. We would talk for twenty or thirty minutes. They were intelligent and wise enough to realize I was not any ordinary worker.

I never tried to take advantage of my growing relationship with the doctors. I enjoyed the stimulating conversation. They often asked my opinion on things or my suggestions for dealing with certain children. In the eyes of the hospital, I was a loyal employee; in their eyes, I was a colleague.

Despite my disappointment and hurt over not being considered for the Director of Marketing position, I always gave 100 percent of my time and energy to my work. I determined to do everything with excellence. Perhaps that's one reason the doctors respected me. Even the marketing director respected me. I was able to be cheerful and to enjoy my work. I decided that hardships and disappointments were not going to define my future.

Even now, as president of Beulah Heights Bible College, I will not allow the position to define who I am. If I can be defined by the college and my position, then my world is limited to what I do for the college. I do believe the vision is larger than myself and Beulah Heights Bible College. That is why I want people to know Beulah Heights and what we are doing rather than knowing Benson. Knowing Benson limits the vision and what God is doing through Beulah Heights for the kingdom.

When people see Benson, they see Beulah Heights. But I want people to know Beulah Heights and where it is heading—not me, because I do believe that I am more than what I am doing now. However, the position I am occupying right now, I give 100 percent of my effort and my attention to do a good job—to leave a legacy. That is me.

With every job, even when I was a janitor, my goal was always to do my best. But I refused to be defined by what I was doing then—and now. I refuse to say, "This is where God wants me for the rest of my life."

Too many people allow themselves to be defined by positions they did not receive or disappointments they encountered. I chose to see all those rejections as transitions for me. If one door did not open, God had a different door through which I should walk. To know that what I am doing right now matters has given me strength and courage along the way. What I am doing right now is building, planting, and investing in tomorrow. So if I invest wrong today, I will reap those things tomorrow. However, if I invest wisely and correctly, I will reap such in the future.

Esther's Illness

I n 1992, my wife became seriously ill. She was in constant pain, and we finally saw the doctor. After he examined her, he referred us to a gynecologist. The gynecologist diagnosed her as having a tumor in her uterus. "She has to have surgery," he told us.

The doctor said it will be an out patient surgery and sent us to South Fulton Hospital on Cleveland Avenue. "We will treat her as an outpatient and she can leave in the afternoon," the nurse informed us.

I did not know much about medicine, but that surprised me.

They did the surgery. I went to begin the process of getting her released from the hospital. Esther whispered, "I'm so cold." She said that several times and her teeth chattered. It was not cold in the room, so I knew something was wrong.

I complained and finally a nurse took her vital signs.

Her blood pressure was extremely low. "Let her wait for a few minutes," the nurse said. She covered Esther with a blanket and left.

At three o'clock they had a shift change and a new nurse came in. "You may take her home now," the new nurse said. "She will be fine." But, she did not take her vital signs again.

"I'm so cold," Esther said, again.

The nurse ignored her and told me to check her out.

I drove Esther back to Beulah Heights. We were living upstairs in the building known as Woods Hall. We had a three-bedroom apartment, and it was much nicer than where we had been during my student days.

There was no elevator, and Esther could not walk up the flight of stairs. "I'm cold and my feet are so heavy," she said.

I stared at her face and I knew she was extremely ill. I did not know what to do. Robin was fourteen years old, but he helped me carry her up the steps. A number of people at the school saw us, but not one of them offered to help. That saddened me greatly. Perhaps I should have asked, but I could not do that. I thought it was obvious we needed help. If they were concerned, they would have done something, or at least offered to help.

Even afterward, no one visited us. Everyone at the school knew about the surgery, but no one helped, visited, or offered to cook food.

For three days Esther could not walk, let alone stand up. I had to help her go to the bathroom and also bathe her. She said, "My feet are so heavy; I can't feel my toes." We did not know what was wrong.

On the third day, she begged, "Please, please call a doctor." I rushed downstairs to the nearest payphone and called her doctor.

I explained to him what was happening and the pain. I was angry and confused. "You told us this is a simple surgery. You said that she can even go back to work within forty-eight hours. But my wife cannot walk. She is not fine. She is telling me she has pain in both legs."

"How long has this been going on?"

"Three days."

"Rush her to the emergency room at the hospital and I will meet you there."

I rushed her back to the emergency room at South Fulton Hospital. The doctor was waiting. I could not go into the surgery room so I sat in the waiting room for nearly four hours. It felt like such a long time, especially with such unknown circumstances.

"She had a blood clot," the doctor said when he came out. "She was very lucky. These things are on both feet on the curve. If you had waited another six hours, you would have lost her."

Esther remained in the hospital for twelve days. In America to be in the hospital for twelve days means that it is quite a serious illness. They gave her blood thinning medication and discharged her. The sickness was no longer life threatening, but she was still quite sick.

I continued working at the hospital and going to college. Esther's illness was a very difficult time for me and the children. I had to do everything for her and prepare the children for school for the next two months. No one ever came in to help, even when I explained our situation.

I am not bitter about the lack of help. It made me realize how much pain and suffering goes on around us all the time and we pay no attention to it.

Of course, the insurance paid most of the hospital bill. However, I still had to pay my co-payment. During the two months Esther did not work, we paid our bills by putting everything on our credit cards. The hospital did set up an easy-payment plan for us. It took us five years to pay off that bill.

When Esther was at South Fulton, we were active members of Beulah Heights Tabernacle, the church loacted on the college campus, I told the pastor but he never visited the hospital. He never sent anyone to see her or me after we came home. No one ever asked about her.

It was difficult not to be bitter. I prayed for God to help me. I was able to remind myself that God was with me. "If I am ever in their position, God, please help me to reach out to those who suffer," I prayed.

I realized then that one day I would reach out. I would do that because I had suffered. And, only those of us who have suffered are acutely aware of the pain of others.

A few people at Beulah Heights Bible College knew about our situation, but hardly anyone ever asked about Esther. Occasionally someone asked, "How can we help you?" I could not bring myself to tell them to bring us food. I usually smiled and thanked them for offering.

There was one exception, a woman named Yvonne Terry. She worked for the college. At that time, she and her husband, Paul, were members of Beulah Heights Tabernacle. One day, she knocked on our door and gave us a whole pot of spaghetti she had cooked. My children were thrilled to have such a large amount to eat at one time.

Paul was wonderful and befriended my children. Many times, they went to Paul's house and he played with them. Sometimes he barbequed and invited them over.

I was not around much of the time because I was studying or I was working at the school. It was not easy to be away from my children. But I truly felt I was doing what God wanted me to do. I am grateful to Paul because he did what I could not do. He became a father-figure to them. He spent time with them. He even showed Robin how to throw a baseball.

Paul and Yvonne stand out so strongly because they were the only ones.

I could not understand the hearts of the other members of Beulah Heights Tabernacle. For example, they had a women's Saturday morning fellowship that included breakfast. During our first two years in Atlanta, I encouraged Esther to go.

She went but never felt comfortable. "You need the exposure," I said. "You need to be with other Christians."

She did for several months, but then she refused to go again. "They act as if I'm not there," she said. She felt rejected and unwanted by the other women. She never returned. Not one woman ever inquired why or asked her back.

That's where Esther and I are different. I can take a lot of rejection and hatred. She's more sensitive and much more quickly hurt when people treat her badly. I was sorry that my wife had to go through so much pain. Much later, I also learned about the pain and rejection my children felt, although they said nothing to me at the time.

Here is an example of life from my family's perspective.

We lived on campus during my student years. There was a basketball hoop and a space to play in the parking lot. By the time the children came from school, the lot was empty. If other students' children played out there, nothing was said. As soon as my children went out to play, the office manager rushed out and said, "You can't play here!"

One day Robin, Peter, and Juliet played basketball and other black children from the neighborhood saw them. And like most kids, they joined them. It was early evening and the service was ready to start at the Tabernacle. The playing area was almost outside the church, which was on school property.

Someone told the office manager, and he rushed outside. He yelled at the children playing, "Who gave you permission to play here?"

They did not answer and ran away. He turned to Robin and asked, "Why did you let them come?"

"I don't know them."

"You know them. You've got to tell me who they are."

"I don't know them."

"I'm going to talk to your dad." He knew I would punish them or tell them not to play there again.

My kids had always said nothing, but this time Robin was angry. "Why do you keep on pushing me? I did not invite them. They came in. How do I know everybody?"

That response really made the office manager angry. He went to our apartment. Esther was there alone because I was working. "You know, I am very disappointed," he said. "Robin invited those neighborhood kids to play on the campus."

Just then, Robin came home and heard the accusation. "I did not invite them. These kids saw us playing basketball and they came and joined us. I am not the security person to tell them to leave. I don't have that authority. They were not doing anything wrong. They were only playing."

I was an employee and I could not say anything. But, Esther had taken enough. She stood up, stared at him, and said, "I'm tired of this. My kids can not even play around in the hallway. People say they can not play there because they are waking them up when they are having naps. They can not play out in the parking lot. Where do you want me to put them? Do you want me to lock these kids in the bathroom? Tell us, what you want us to do? When your grandkids visit, do you lock them inside somewhere? I see them playing around in the parking lot and you do not stop them."

She really stood up to him. I would not have had the courage to do so.

He walked out and slammed the door; however, after that day, he never again talked roughly to our children.

● ● ● ● ●

Five years later, in 1997, Esther became ill again. Another tumor had grown and they had to remove it.

At that time, it was easier because I had insurance with Kaiser Permanente. They sent us to Atlanta's Northside Hospital. She was in the hospital three days before they would release her to go home. Kaiser also provided cheaper prices for the medication.

It was summer and we had to stop on the way home so I could buy the prescription drugs. We did not have air conditioning, so I did not leave the car running. When I returned, I saw people surrounding our car.

"What's going on?" I asked.

"Bleeding," Esther said. The hospital had let her go even though she was not well enough. Also, they had given her Coumadin, which is a blood-thinning medication. She was bleeding badly.

We had stopped at Kaiser near Northlake Mall to pick up some medicine. I went upstairs to pick up the medicine. When I reached the car, an African-American man was holding Esther and blood seemed to be pouring from all over her body. He was wearing a white shirt. Her blood soaked it everywhere, but he never complained. He helped me get her back inside the clinic.

Several people who had grouped around thought she was giving birth, but of course, I knew better. I almost fell down. They removed the bloody clothing and put her in a hospital paper gown and told me to return her to Northside Hospital. This was a very stupid idea. At four-thirty in the afternoon in Atlanta and on I-285, this was a crazy idea. I had no energy to argue. I was confused and scared. I did not think of calling an ambulance.

"She should not have been discharged," the staff at Kaiser said.

I said I would take Esther. My children were with me. They squeezed into the front seat and Esther was in the backseat, crying and groaning. She wore nothing but that paper gown. It was four-thirty and I drove up I-285 in the midst of all the going-home traffic.

I thought, if I have to drive through this traffic, I will lose my wife. Why didn't they call an ambulance?

I decided that whether police arrested me or not, I was going to drive on the shoulder of the road and pass the cars. I put on my hazard lights and drove as fast as I could. The police did not stop me and no one tried to block me. I soon reached Northside Hospital.

No doctor or nurse was willing to see her.

If she had come to the hospital in an ambulance, she would have received immediate attention. So I grabbed a wheelchair and helped Esther into it. We started straight through to the ER.

"You can't go in there," someone yelled, but I kept going. No one was going to stop my wife from getting immediate treatment.

Anyone could see the blood all over her and that she was in bad shape. They allowed me to pass.

A woman doctor, who was from India, examined her and stitched her up. "I'm going to let her go now," she said. "She's okay."

"She is not all right," I protested. "She has been released twice from this hospital. Both times, I almost lost her." I kept my voice calm but firm, "Do you want me to lose my wife?"

"I'm sorry," the doctor said. "I'll admit her."

They put Esther in a room and kept her for three days. The first doctor who came to her room agreed that she needed to be kept there.

Those two incidents taught me how difficult it can be for strangers in this country, especially the first time when we had no health insurance.

"God, you are with us," I said many times. "This is what gives me strength."

By the time Esther was in the hospital at Northside Hospital in 1997, we were members of North Avenue Presbyterian Church. I told Dr. Prak and he visited her immediately.

Several others from the church came as well. What a difference in churches! Beulah Heights Tabernacle had perhaps
40 members and the pastor never visited us once. No one
reached out to us. North Avenue Presbyterian Church had
at least a thousand members. Several visited us and many
cared. We appreciated the love and concern from the Body
of Christ.

12

Moving Up at Beulah Heights

M y office was shifted once again. This time, they moved me to the library. That was alright because I still helped in the library—at no payment, of course, just as a volunteer.

The librarian had retired from the public library. Her name was Mary. She had a degree in Library Science, and I assisted her. She was fine to work with. One of the accrediting conditions for the college was that after receiving full accreditation, they would have to hire a full-time librarian with a Master of Library Science degree.

Mary was not able to work full-time. No one else on staff had the academic qualifications to take that position. I realized the situation and knew how I could help. Even though I had planned to study for my doctorate, I diverted from it. I decided to spend eighteen months to earn a

Master of Library Science degree.

I don't know why I did that except that I felt it was my calling and my duty to the college.

My wife supported everything I did, but she also had some reservations. "You are not making enough money for all that you are doing now."

"You are right," I said, "but this is something I believe God wants me to do."

I enrolled at Clark Atlanta University and worked hard until I completed my M.L.S. degree. After I received my degree, I became the full-time librarian plus I was still the part-time Fiscal Officer.

The school raised my salary to $17,000 per year. They also gave me medical benefits—which they never had given me before. I resigned from the hospital.

One day a woman from the office came to see me in the library. She stood around, browsed among the books, and finally started to talk. "We run this place. You know that, don't you? Don't think there is anybody else running this place. We are running it."

Her words shocked me. I had no advance warning about how she felt. Later, I assumed she felt my coming on staff threatened her husband's position of authority in the areas of finance.

"I'm sure you do," I said.

"Do you know that you can be fired?"

"I know that. I know that I can be fired."

She smiled and started to walk away.

I spoke once more. "But do you understand one thing? This college belongs to God and not to one person? Today, you are here and the day will come when you will not be here. Today, I am here and the day will come when I will not be here."

I had been at Beulah Heights Bible College for approximately five years. It was the first time I had ever spoken up like that. I decided to say what I wanted to say, even if I may have been fired. "Don't you understand this thing is bigger than both of us?"

She started to laugh. It was a laugh of embarrassment. I think she had not expected any such answer from me. I had always kept silent and did what she and the others in the office told me to do.

After she walked away, I asked, "Lord, what am I doing here? I have two masters' degrees, and I can get a job anywhere. She doesn't have a degree in anything and neither does the office manager. Why am I here?"

As soon as I prayed those words, I knew the answer. I loved Sam Chand and I felt a keen sense of loyalty to him. Dr. Chand had shown me respect. I felt my obligation to deny myself and my problem so that I could support him to accomplish his goals of building the college.

13

Growing In Humility

I have already mentioned that Dr. Chand was influential in my life and how much I love and respect him. There is one incident that I want to share. He did a kind and simple gesture that opened my heart to him.

One very hot summer day when I was a student and a janitor, I was cleaning the bathroom in the women's dormitory. The dorm had no air conditioning. The shower place was built on concrete about four or six inches deep. It was seriously clogged by hair, soap, and other stuff. By the smell, I assumed it had been stopped for more than three days. There were only four girls in the dorm at that time.

A female student came to report the clogged drain while I was in the administration building. The office manager told me to go and unclog the drain. I did not have any knowledge about plumbing. However, I rented what they call a snake—the roto rooter that is put down pipes.

When I opened the door to do my work, the smell nauseated me. I opened the door to let in some air, but the smell was so bad, it reached all the way to the administration building.

Within minutes, my entire body was covered with perspiration. I was also frustrated. I asked one of the women, "Why did you let this get so bad?"

"We reported it to the office manager weeks ago."

He had not said a word. The situation had worsened. I wondered why they did not get a professional plumber to do the job. After perhaps an hour, I got rid of the debris and the water started to flow through again.

While I was working, Sam walked by, looked inside, and saw me working. He did not say a word but turned and left. When he returned a minute later, he carried a large glass of water and handed it to me.

As I drank, I saw tears in his eyes.

I drank every bit of water and handed back the empty glass. "Thank you."

He took the glass and walked away.

This simple incident became a defining moment. His love and his compassion showed through greater than any words he could ever have spoken.

I'll never forget that man. He has done so many things for me. But that glass of water is the one thing I can never forget. It meant a lot to me that the president of the school would care. My immediate supervisor did not even come to see what I was doing.

Such experiences taught me how to appreciate the good things God sends my way. Through those early years at Beulah Heights Bible College, God taught me how to treat people fairly. It taught me as a leader and now I regularly ask myself two questions. When I ask people to do something, is it something I would do? Can I be fair to the people I lead?

When I finished the work on the drain and I washed myself, I sat there and cried. I was perplexed. I prayed, "God help me that I'll never again go through this process that I went through today. But if I have to do it, if it is Your will, I'll do it. But help me never to go through this process ever again."

I knew that hate, discrimination, and prejudice had me do that stuff, knowing that I was not a professional plumber.

I wondered if they loved me as the woman in the office had said. If she loved me, would she have threatened me in the same breath? Many times she had said she loved me almost as if I were her own son. But then the prejudice would come through.

For example, as my children were growing up, in the summertime they would play basketball outside in back of Woods Hall. They were in middle school and other black kids from the neighborhood would come to shoot hoops.

The office manager would come out and yell, "No. You can't play here."

"Okay, they can't play but can we play?" My children and Pradeep's son (Dr. Chand's brother-in-law) would ask. The office manager would refuse them because they allowed those kids from the neighborhood.

Any day the office manager's grandchildren came, they seemed to do anything they wanted. They would play, throw football—even break glass. But, he never punished them.

I got along fine with him. But it meant that I could do so only as long as I stayed under his domination and showed him the servant-to-master attitude. I continued to pray for God's help. When I realized the man was not educated, I realized he lived in a very small world. I was educated and that must have intimidated him. I was getting promotions and he was still doing the same things he had always done.

His management style was to oppress people like me. I have known of dictators like that in Africa, such as the notorious Idi Amin of Uganda—an ignorant and bloodthirsty dictator. Amin was a bully and he killed his enemies.

I don't mean to compare Amin and the office manager, but their tactics were similar—both bullied and were men of low self-esteem. Neither knew how to earn respect; both knew only how to grab and demand it.

I came to realize that the office manager did not care about the educational degrees. He never went to college. Once I grasped that, I felt sorry for him, and once I felt sorry for him, I could truly show him love.

Did those people in the office know what they were doing? Probably not. It is something that's in them. We were the first black people to start growing up there. We brought in more black people. Before long, there were more students and staff of color from around the world than there were white students.

I learned that I must not fight the system in the wrong way. That is one of the mistakes people make when they think that they have to fight things — to win such a war, we have to behave differently.

Bruce Lee, the former Kung-Fu fighter, said that whenever he fought with his enemy he started to think like the enemy. He also said that he took on the shape of water. Water has no shape. If we pour water into a glass, it takes the shape of the glass. If we pour the liquid into a cup, it takes the shape. He had to learn to be like them in order to win.

I had to do that. I don't mean feel the prejudice. But, I had to learn where they were coming from. Why did they think the way they did? It's like boxing. Once I understand the opponent's style, I'll know when he's going to throw a punch with his left hand or right. I encountered a lot of bullying. I was the Fiscal Officer as well as the Librarian. Therefore, technically, I was in charge of the library. I had to make decisions such as whether we needed additional shelving, and if so, should it be new or used shelving. But I did not have the authority to make the purchase; I had to go through somebody else.

That helped me understand how bureaucracy works. I could work today in any government because I understand how carefully we have to maneuver around those who have authority but no insight. That's why some people get discouraged; they spend their energies fighting the system but accomplish nothing.

I got around the prejudice and the power struggles in the office by using a strategy that I learned from Dr. John Maxwell. When he became the pastor of Skyline in San Diego, his first church, he was quite young. At the first meeting with the board, he realized he was not the leader. He was only the preacher. Several elders controlled everything the board did. He had to work through them to get the work done.

Maxwell helped me to understand that for me now to accomplish what I wanted done, I had to make such people my friends—even for them to think of themselves as important and intelligent.

Let's take the office manager for example. Although I was the Fiscal Officer, he was in charge of the finances. He had control over the money before I came and I knew it was useless to fight him to relinquish any authority. He was running things and I had to learn to work with him.

Instead of fighting, I listened to him and he loved to talk. He loved to be told how important he was. That's when I knew how to take on the shape of water.

I had decided that the library really needed more shelving capacity. I realized that if I went and asked for money to make the changes, I would get ten minutes of lecture on reasons why the school did not have the money to buy new shelving. I determined not to make that mistake.

One morning, I was in his office. We chatted a few minutes. Just before I was ready to leave I said, "By the way, I'd like your opinion on something." I took him down to the library and showed him the shelving challenges. "I've been thinking about adding shelves, but I'd like your advice. What do you think?" I explained things as simply as possible, but saying as little as possible so the result would be his idea.

"If you are going to put shelves over there, you need good, solid wood," he said.

"Wouldn't plywood work?" I knew the answer, of course.

He laughed and shook his head. "No, no. Plywood would not be suitable," he stated.

"What kind of shelves would work?" I asked—as if I had absolutely no idea. I had also learned that he loved to shop. So he started talking about the prices at various stores.

"Really? Is there that much difference?"

"Oh yes, and you have to be good at knowing that kind of thing or they'll cheat you every time."

"What kind of shelves would work best in here?"

He started to explain everything to me about the differences in the quality. He almost sounded like a contractor.

"Can you draw it for me? Could you help me plan it? Would you mind doing that?"

"Of course, I'll be glad to help." Within minutes, he had figured out exactly the right size of shelves, how much wood we would need, and he was almost certain he knew the best place to buy what was needed. He drew me a picture of the shelving and stayed busy at it for several hours. He became very excited about the project.

Then he said, "Let's go talk to Dr. Chand." I followed him into the president's office. "We need to buy shelves for the library. We've run out of space for books." He made a big presentation about why we needed new shelving. He explained what it would look like and how much it would cost.

Unless Sam directly asked me a question, I never said a word. He may have figured out what I was doing; I am not sure. It did not matter to me who received credit for the idea. But, it did matter to me that we had new shelves.

New shelving had become the project of the office manager and no longer mine.

We had new shelving within two days.

One time we wanted to expand the library—we just had to do that. The accrediting agency informed us that we had to provide seating capacity for at least 25 percent of our student body. The only way we could do that was to take over one of the classrooms and change it into a library seating area.

I went in to see the office manager and we talked quite a bit. At first, however, I was not quite so persuasive. He could not understand why we had to expand the library. "That will cost money," he said, "and I don't think we should be spending that kind of money just to expand the library."

I kept talking and asking his advice. I thought he finally understood. I expected he would support what we had to do and might even claim it as his own idea.

Both of us went in to see Dr. Chand. Immediately, to my surprise, he switched positions. "This is just too much money. We should not spend money on the library when we have more important needs around here."

"But we have to do this," I insisted. That was not wise of me but I was frustrated. "If we are going to be accredited, we have to expand."

"No. We won't do it," he said.

"I thought we talked about this," I said and I explained.

"No, we did not talk," he said, "and we are not going to do it."

"Just a minute," Dr. Chand said. "Benson, help me understand this correctly. Expansion is something we must do if we are going to be accredited?"

"Yes, it is," I said.

"Then we do it."

The office manager walked away angry. I did not gloat. I knew that although I had won, it would make the next battle more difficult. I prayed and asked God to soften his heart.

I don't know what happened after that, but the next day the office manager came to see me. "I should not have acted that way and I am sorry," he said.

I made it clear that I was fine and held nothing against

him. And I didn't. I was glad that God had answered my prayer and we had resolved the issue. I did not want our relationship to be difficult. I did not want to dwell on the negatives; I chose to focus on the journey of preparing myself for whatever leadership role God had for me in the future.

Those years were years of great education—not just in the classroom, but practical learning to deal with ignorant and obstinate people. I had to learn to cope with those multiple personalities within the leaders and move ahead. I could never forget that I was an immigrant and that others would always regard me that way.

By that time, I started to work full-time in the library. Dr. Chand approved that the college would help me apply for a green card. This helped me take different positions in the college without the concern of a work permit. It took about three years for me to receive my green card.

I had the green card before I completed my doctorate. Then Dr. Chand promoted me to the position of Vice President and Fiscal Officer of Beulah Heights Bible College.

I have thought about my journey quite often. For somebody to leave Africa, go to the United States and endure that kind of process takes a lot of wisdom from God. I had to learn what I could and could not do. I had to learn the lifestyle, personalities, and different leadership styles prevalent in the United States.

When I became the Fiscal Officer of the college, I had the sense that together Dr. Chand and I could do anything.

For example, we were approved to award federal financial aid. Our first federal financial aid check was $20,000. The school had never before received that large a sum in a single check.

I was really excited. At the time the money came, there was an administrative meeting in session between the office manager, Dr. Keiller, and Dr. Chand.

I ran to the office and knocked on the door. Dr. Chand told me to come in.

"Guys, I have a check." I held it up and said, "It is for $20,000."

I expected that they would have grabbed me and hugged me or shout praise to God.

"What do we do with it?" the office manager asked. He started on some kind of rampage that shocked me badly. "How are we going to disperse the money?"

"It is money for reimbursement," I said, but, he did not understand what that meant. "We do not have a choice on how to disperse the money. The government has done that." I tried to explain that we had to deposit the check in the college account and then we would disburse the money to the students." He did not understand the terminology.

"Why do we have to give students the money?" he asked. "The check is made out to the school."

"We can't withhold the checks for students from the federal government."

I am not sure he ever understood what I was trying to say, but Sam caught on. He tried to explain it to the office manager. I am still not sure Sam got through to him.

When I walked out of the meeting, I had mixed feelings. If it had not been for Dr. Chand speaking up, I am not sure where the meeting would have gone.

Dr. Chand is an encourager and a man of much energy. He loves people and has the heart of a pastor. He is also an immigrant and understands many of the things I had endured. This is not the place to write about Sam's own rejections and the prejudice against him. He suffered in many ways. One thing I respect about him as a leader is that he never called me into his office and told me what was going on with the people who opposed me. I never sat with him—ever—and talked about other leaders. He would have never allowed that. If he knew a mistake or mistreatment had taken place, he would do what he could to correct it—and correct it quickly. His example helped me to understand the importance of never talking with my staff against any leader.

I learned to deal with the rejection by understanding that the rejection is only part of the issue. There are underlying factors. I also realized that rejection today is not rejection forever. This is temporary and I will have the opportunity to try again.

Rejection to Vice President

A s mentioned previously, we went to Beulah Heights Tabernacle when we first arrived in Atlanta. Located on the edge of the school property, it had seen better days and the small church was slowly dying. They had no programs for children, and we had no transportation. So we decided to attend there. The people were quite poor, although we did not know that at the time. We had just come from Africa and almost everyone in the United States seemed wealthy to us.

We stayed with that church for six years. That was probably a mistake; we should have left as soon as we had a car. We thought of going to other churches almost from the beginning, but in those days we were pressured to attend that church unless we already had connections with another local church.

We became active at Beulah Heights Tabernacle. I decided to pray this way, "God, if You want people to help us, lay it on their hearts to do so, we will not ask." After six years and one final rejection, we moved our membership to North Avenue Presbyterian Church which is in the downtown area of Atlanta.

There were several reasons why we chose to move. The first and the one that bothered me the most was the fact that Beulah Heights Tabernacle had nothing to offer my children. There were no youth programs and I sensed no motivation to start any. Secondly, I do not intend to be judgmental but I sensed that the members had a limited world view. They were like a small group of people who wanted to keep the world out and had no interest or energy to invite people inside. The third reason was what finally made me know it was time to leave. It happened like this. The leaders of the church called me one Saturday. "We would like you to serve as one of our elders. We are having elections Sunday afternoon and we would like to know if you would want to serve."

"Sure, I'd love to do that. I'd love to serve. I've been here for more than five years and I'd like to do it."

My family and I went to the meeting that afternoon. It started at four o'clock. I waited and finally, they announced the names of the elders they had nominated. The congregation was then asked to voice them in and they did.

I was not one of those people mentioned.

No one called my name.

No one, not then not ever. They didn't even have the courtesy to tell me that they had withdrawn my name.

I felt rejected. It was the most painful rejection I had experienced since coming to Beulah Heights Tabernacle.

Later I realized that I should not have been surprised.

I thought of how long it had taken for me to become a full member. I applied for membership within a few weeks after our family began attending. It is interesting that the office manager and the district overseer were the same person.

I waited a few weeks and asked about membership. "It is somewhere in the office," he said. "We just have not gotten around to it." Nearly two years passed before they finally voted me in as a full member. *Two years!*

Why was I surprised at what they had done about voting me in as an elder?

They had dwindled to forty people and later disbanded altogether. My weakness in that ordaining part was that I am loyal to people. That's why I stuck with Dr. Chand when I could have done so much more for my career elsewhere. But Sam was the man who helped me apply for my green card when he became aware that I did not have one. There was a genuine connection and friendship between Sam and me. Because of loyalty to Sam and thus to Beulah Heights Bible College, I also gave that same loyalty to Beulah Heights Tabernacle. My children really wanted to go elsewhere, but I was the one who kept us there.

I learned that Sunday afternoon that loyalty can sometimes be a handicap. That Sunday evening I made a decision and said to myself, "I must leave this church. I must move where I can serve and be respected."

When I told Esther she said, "Praise the Lord!" She did not ask, "What took you so long?" and I appreciated that.

I did not leave immediately. Perhaps that was just stubbornness. No one ever came and explained. There were rumors that the pastor, one of the members or the district overseer would not allow a black man to serve. I never knew the real reason and it no longer mattered. That was the time I made the decision to go. I had to move on to something else.

Later, I told Dr. Chand about my rejection and he laughed. He knew what was happening. He had never spoken a word against anyone there, even though some of those same people had rejected him—an Indian—when he wanted to marry Brenda, a white girl.

There is a footnote to this story. I was appointed president of Beulah Heights Bible College in 2004. Shortly after that I received a letter from the general secretary of the International Pentecostal Church of Christ. Beulah Heights Bible College has been an integral part of that organization, although the school has more than 45 denominations represented. I had been humiliated in 1992 and eleven years later, the secretary wrote me a letter and apologized for that incident. Apparently, somebody knew and remembered. It is also interesting that the general secretary is related to one of the women who worked in the office and was part of the power structure of the Tabernacle.

I do not think I had ever felt so rejected in my life. I knew then that I would leave Beulah Heights Tabernacle but I did not want to leave with bitterness. I wanted to leave with a calm and forgiving spirit which is probably the reason why I waited.

When I told Dr. Keiller and Dr. Chand that I was moving my membership, Dr. Keiller said he thought it was a good idea.

"I would never go to that church," Sam said. "So, I think you can understand how I feel."

I did understand and I knew the history of his rejection. In all the years I had worked with him at Beulah Heights, not once did he ever try to pollute me or to speak against the people of that church. He did not want to tell me. He wanted me to learn by myself.

We started attending North Avenue Presbyterian Church. Esther had grown up in the Presbyterian Church. I knew more about the Presbyterian Church than any of the others, even though I was raised in the African Inland Church (AIC). Most of the American AIC missionaries were Baptist. The African Inland Church and the Presbyterian Church governments are quite similar. I felt more comfortable.

North Avenue Presbyterian Church had programs for youth and young children and Dr. Jim Long was the pastor. Dr. Prakobb Deetanna was on staff as the minister to international students. He was originally from Thailand. He was never very articulate in English but he was a warm and solid leader. Dr. Deetanna also became a good friend. He had become a staff member at North Avenue Presbyterian Church when it was all white. He understood the challenges and how to work past the prejudices. Prak helped me in my journey through Beulah Heights.

Prak stayed on the staff through five senior pastors. For someone to survive five senior pastors demonstrates true leadership. He knew his line. He knew how to toe his line.

Our children had heard about places such as Disney World or Whitewater Rapids since our early days in Atlanta, but we could never afford to take them. To their credit, the children did not beg because they soon learned that we did not have the money to do such things.

Immediately after we moved our membership to North Avenue Presbyterian Church, my children joined the youth group. The groups often went to Disney World or took a trip to Mexico. Most of the time the church paid all the expenses. So, our children went places we could never afford to send them.

By then God had begun to smile on us and bring many blessings into our lives.

Through a woman I met at North Avenue Presbyterian Church, someone from Coca Cola called me. They offered me an excellent opportunity. I would be making more money than I had ever thought possible.

I was ready to say yes.

But once again, Dr. Samuel Chand intervened. He did

not know about the offer from Coca Cola.

He came into my office one day and said, "Benson, I need your help. I've decided to appoint you to the position of Vice President of Student Affairs. "

Once again, it seemed as if God had whispered to him. He did not know I had been considering a change in employment.

It always seemed as if God was sitting there with him, telling him that things were about to change. Only three years after I became vice president did I tell him.

I had another significant job offer and it was again very appealing. I applied for the position as Director of Development for the DeKalb County School System. DeKalb County is the most populated and the largest out of the five major counties in metro Atlanta. They offered to pay me a large amount of money for the job.

I was still struggling over whether to accept the DeKalb County position when Dr. Chand, who again knew nothing of this, came into my office. He had just returned from Kenya. This was his second day back in the office and he wanted to speak with me.

"We can help the church in Kenya," he said "And I need you to work with me. I've given them thirteen full scholarships. Besides that, I want you to lead a team every summer to go to Kenya and train leaders there."

I stared at him, hardly able to believe what I heard. I could go back and visit my own country. I could invest in the life of the church and especially in developing leaders.

That was far more rewarding than all the money from Coca Cola or DeKalb County.

I turned down both positions.

The thought of becoming a missionary to my own country was incredible. I was excited to think that I would have an opportunity to help people who have no voice and no opportunity to experience a different life. I was overwhelmed with the idea that I could touch my country in a more significant way than I could at Coca Cola.

I realized that I would have an opportunity to affect change quicker than other missionaries because I already understood the culture, the people, and their needs. Had I chosen Coca Cola, I would have limited myself and the scope of possibilities would have been restricted to the corporate world. Working with Dr. Chand would allow me to help leaders and missionaries understand that Kenyan people are not stupid, as the former missionaries assumed. We just have a different way of life and culture. I could assist in bridging the gap to a better understanding and partnership with others.

We established the African American Consortium of Theological Studies (AACTS). This organization has been partnering with church and business leaders to influence cultural barriers and empower the people in Africa as communities are changed one by one.

• • • • •

In 1994, Esther was hurt at work. She had lifted a heavy child and it injured her back. At times, she still experiences pain today. Esther had to go to physical therapy but could not stop working. It saddened me to see her in pain. We needed the one hundred dollars she earned a week to pay our bills.

She did not complain. Esther knew what she had to do.

Although I was at peace, many times I asked God why life had to be so hard on my dear wife.

We learned many things about saving money after we moved to the United States. Whenever possible we bought in bulk. Or I would go to the Farmers Market and buy a whole box of wings or chicken legs. Until about 2001, I bought all my clothes from outlet stores and thrift stores. To this day I always watch for bargains. We purchased the best we could afford. That was an excellent experience for me. I came from wealth and prestige in Nakuru to being impoverished in Atlanta. Like Joseph, who had been rejected by his brothers, I was able to see that God was in everything. Even during my worst times I knew that they would not last forever.

I now see that God stripped away any pride I had. Few people knew how much we suffered. Esther and I decided we would not tell people our needs. That was not pride on our part but rather an expression of our determination to trust God to provide for our needs.

We had to learn to help ourselves no matter how little we had. For instance, even today I could take twenty dollars and go to a thrift store. I would come out with a suit for $8 and a blazer for $2.50. I would take both of them to the dry cleaners and bring home what looked like new clothes.

This is important because too many people want to start at the top. I have met too many immigrants, who come to this country and hold out their hands to receive. They do not know how to get out of that pattern.

Shortly before we moved our membership to North Avenue, I bought a nice 1995 Nissan. Although nothing like a Cadillac or an Acura, it was a nice looking car.

One of my immigrant friends said "You should not drive that nice car to North Avenue."

"Why not, is there something wrong with it?"

"You don't want to show those people that you can buy a good car."

"Why don't I?, I did not borrow anybody's money. I bought it myself."

My friend and I talked quite a while before he realized that we did not need to come looking poor. Once I began to drive a nice car, other immigrants also did the same thing.

One of them told me, "If I look poor, they will give me money." One man gave me $100. Another time I received a new suit for Christmas."

I did not want that and I told Esther, "I don't want to go to a church because I want to receive something from the people. I want to go there to worship with people."

I urged international students not to become tourists

in church, looking for good scenes so that they can take photos. Go to worship God and in the process of worshipping God, the blessings will come. Somebody will see you and may help you, but most of them won't."

I know how that works because I have heard so many stories from other immigrants. They go and expect help. When no one offers, they leave disappointed. The problem is that they get used to receiving something. They are like bears. If we go into the woods and feed the bears during the summer, then they will depend on that food. When winter comes no one brings food, they will have forgotten how to forage for themselves and only know how to depend on others. They wait to receive and when nothing comes, they die. If they learn to hunt for themselves it will not matter what season of the year it is, they will be able to take care of themselves. Someone may feed them and they will eat but they will not depend on it.

That is the kind of leader I am trying to train.

There are two immigrant students that come to my mind. I told them, "Don't look for what you can get, show what you can give them." These two students followed my advice.

The first is Juma who is from Kitale in Western Kenya. When he first came to the school I said to him, "May I advise you?" "When you go to a church, go to worship the true God. Do not worship people or look for those who will help you. Be sincere and as transparent as you can. Before you end your education, you will have planted seeds. You may not get to see the plants grow, but don't be discouraged."

"And don't be discouraged because some of your friends go to a different church and may receive $500. You may want to go there too but don't. Hang out where you can worship. If they help you with money that is fine. If they don't, that is also fine."

Juma listened. I believed he would follow through. He joined a church in the downtown area of Atlanta. He attended faithfully and people noticed.

One day the pastor of that church called me. "We need to hire somebody to open the church on Wednesday, to turn off the lights on Sunday evening, and to do a few things around here and there." "Is there a student who would do that?" "We would pay him. There is also an apartment that is adjacent to the church. The person can live there for free. We might even be able to give them a stipend. We do not know these students well." "Could you recommend someone?" "Who should we ask?"

At that time, I was the Vice President for Student Services and I dealt with international students all the time.

"There is a gentleman here who used to be a pastor in Kenya," the pastor said. "His name is Juma and he attends your school. Please tell me a little about him."

"I know Juma," I said.

"Is he someone who can be trusted with the facility?", they asked.

I said, "Absolutely! Juma also works here as a maintenance person. We know him well and we respect him. He has been faithful in his work and in his studies."

Juma received the job and an apartment.

One day he talked to members of the Sunday school

class. One of the elders asked, "Juma, what would you want to do?"

He replied, "I'm trying to finish this school then I will do two years to earn a master's degree. After that, I will go home. My dream is to be at a church." He opened his heart and told them of his dream when he returned to Kenya.

Until then, no one realized how serious he was about returning and ministering in Africa.

"How much would that church cost that you want to do?" the elder asked.

"Probably about $50,000 or something," Juma answered.

The man nodded and said nothing more.

Three years later after Juma finished his education, he was ready to return to Kitali. The church held a special service of appreciation for him and raised $28,000 for him.

The elder to whom he had talked to three years earlier, asked him, "You once said you wanted to return to build a church and you estimated it would cost $50,000."

Juma smiled. "And you remembered that?"

"Yes, I remembered. I have watched you. I want you to go back to Kenya, build that church and then I will come and see what you have done." Before Juma could say anything, He then added, "I'm going to write a check for $65,000 for the church."

Juma could hardly believe it and started to cry.

He did not know that the pastor had called me. "We're trying to give this money to Juma. Do you think he can do it?"

I said, "If you trusted him to work at the church and he did everything you asked, why would he be different now?"

When Juma returned to Kitali, he had almost $90,000 to build a church. God honored his faithfulness.

The second student I want to mention is Zachariah, another man from Kenya. After he enrolled at Beulah Heights Bible College, he began to attend a Four Square Church in Stockbridge, Georgia called Living Way located on the south side of Atlanta. He came to me because he saw some of his classmates bring in money and gifts from various churches. He was tempted to do the same thing but he asked me about it.

"Don't do that I said. Be humble and serve in any way you can. Let the people see your love for Jesus Christ. Let your faith shine."

When Zachariah returned to Kenya, that church raised $75,000 for him. They took a team to Kenya, bought property for him, and helped him get a church started. Three years after his return Zachariah had a congregation of more than 3,000 members.

Zachariah's faithfulness inspired the students in the chapel to raise $5,000 to buy him a car. "We give you something little now and people get tired. Or, you can look for long term goals and forget these little things that you are going to get here. Think about what is going to happen in the future. Focus on the big picture."

God honors those who are faithful to Him. When He provides the dream He also arranges for the resources.

The Waiting
Pays Off

M y beloved friend, Dr. Prakobb Deetanna, died in
2004. Three of the four surviving pastors came to
the funeral. One of them said, "If there is any one who was
Godly, it was Prak. If there was anyone who was Christlike,
it was Prak."

I closed my eyes and nodded. I could easily echo those
words. Prak taught me many valuable lessons. He taught
me how to maneuver myself through the giants. He taught
me as a leader how to survive when the odds were against
me. That is a very significant factor about leadership. It
does not matter what industry we are in; we have to know
how to survive.

Too many people think leaders stay on top because they
fight and defeat their enemies. I do not agree. We stay on
top because we disarm our enemies and stop the fighting.

This is known as diplomacy.

Dr. Chand reminds me that even when I am disappointed with someone or with a situation, I am to use diplomacy. I want the other person to know where I stand on a situation. For instance, as president, I have the authority to fire anyone but I prefer to talk it over and either let them fire themselves or make serious changes.

When I moved my membership to North Avenue Presbyterian Church in 1993, they welcomed us and made us feel at home. Esther worked for a day-care center teaching Pre-K for the state government of Georgia and was finally making enough money to be a financial help.

We became American citizens in 1997. We could have applied earlier, as soon as we had lived in the United States for five years but for the first few years we assumed we would return to Kenya. The longer we stayed in Atlanta and the longer I worked for Beulah Heights Bible College, the more convinced both Esther and I became that God wanted us to become citizens.

After we moved our membership to North Avenue Presbyterian Church and because of the rejection that I had received at Beulah Heights Tabernacle, I did not want any leadership role. I wanted to go there, attend service, and sit on the back row.

Rejection can change us and make us bitter if we are not careful. It can destroy our self-esteem. If we experience rejection often enough, we are constantly afraid someone will do something to us or reject us again. For a time, I felt like the teenage boy who approaches a girl for a dance and he gets turned down. He gets turned down by a second girl. Rather than get rejected a third time, he just stays home. I did not want to stay home but I was too hurt to press forward.

I attended the international Sunday school class and I sat there for several weeks. Nobody knew what I was doing. By then I was Vice President of Beulah Heights Bible College but I was there to attend church and nothing else.

Prak would not allow me to just sit. He kept pushing me to do something. I slowly opened up and began to help when asked. The big change came when the people at North Avenue Presbyterian Church wanted me to serve as president of the international Sunday school class which is one of the largest Sunday school classes in the church. Prak sent me to several mission works in various countries.

Eventually, the nomination committee asked me to serve as an elder. I had been at that church long enough that I knew I was not going to be treated as I had been in the past, so I said yes. The congregation of 1,200 people voted for me to become an elder. Once I was elected, the session (church board) asked me to serve on this committee. I was the first of a few blacks to serve on the finance committee.

The following year I headed the stewardship committee. Again, I was the first black person to serve on that committee as well. The stewardship committee raises money for the projected budget. The people responded to me—and there had been some doubt in my mind whether they would.

During the stewardship campaign, we met the budget and raised almost two million dollars.

I have stayed active at North Avenue Presbyterian Church since late 1993. After I became President of Beulah Heights Bible College in 2004, I resigned from several committees. I knew I would be very busy and felt that I needed to focus on that responsibility.

For a church like North Avenue Presbyterian Church to put me in such a leadership position was very encouraging. As an elder and as chair of the stewardship committee, I was not only encouraged, built character and confidence. I truly felt honored to be trusted by the people at North Avenue.

Another great blessing to me at North Avenue Presbyterian Church was the exposure to different types of people. When I was a student at Beulah Heights Bible College and a member of Beulah Heights Tabernacle, I dealt with people who had no education or very little exposure to diversity. They seemed unaware of their lack of education yet they needed to feel important.

I kept thinking of how different it was to serve at North Avenue. I met a number of wealthy people. They made nothing of their wealth and did not talk about their achievements. They were also people who cared about the community and were often the largest donors when the appeal came to help needy causes. Those men exemplified a type of leadership to which I had little exposure since coming to the United States.

I felt I was thrust into a unique position because I have known what it is like to be an immigrant, to work and live among African Americans. I know what it is like to feel prejudice and belittled just because of my ethnic background. I have also known the other side—the white church. I have worked with the poor and ignorant and alongside the wealthiest and most powerful. I understand the challenges internationals experience. So for me, it puts me in a very unique position that I am able to bridge these three groups together.

At Beulah Heights Bible College, I am able to greet and talk with international students and let the Americans understand what they are going through. I have been able to say to internationals, "Don't think that when Americans say certain things it means they hate you. Think of them as ignorant and perhaps frightened. Ignorant does not mean stupid; it means they do not have information."

As I have explained, too often we respond by assumption. We need to be careful to think things through, and not make decisions based purely on emotional responses.

In some ways, it is amazing to be where I am. When I joined North Avenue Presbyterian Church, many of the members did not know much about Pentecostal churches and could not understand why we had colleges. They know now. They have learned to trust me and they have seen the help they have been able to offer the colleges and students.

Since 1997, North Avenue Presbyterian Church has contributed and supported Beulah Heights Bible College. North Avenue Presbyterian Church has become partners with Beulah Heights Bible College and many African American churches, especially on mission projects.

When Dr. Prak retired in 2001, Dr. Scott Weimer the senior pastor of North Avenue Presbyterian Church approached me. He asked if I would consider taking this position if offered.

Scott Weimer is not only my pastor, he is also my friend. We were able to sit and talk freely. If there is anybody who has invested in my life, it is Scott. He is a loving and dedicated leader. I sometimes call him and we have lunch. Or, I go to see him and I can freely empty my heart to him.

"If I take this position," I told Scott, "I am going to limit myself. I would be here to serve North Avenue and the Presbyterian Church. Right now, what I am doing at Beulah Heights Bible College means I can serve Beulah Heights, North Avenue, New Birth Missionary Baptist Church, Bishop Long, and many other denominations because I am not limited. I am not in a box. I can take a mission team to South Africa, Brazil, and Kenya. I am able to take others and everyone is alright with working with other denominations.

But if I come to North Avenue, you would not allow me to do all of that. I would of course, focus on building up the Presbyterian Church. Because for me, that is limiting.

Scott nodded. It was obvious he understood my perspective.

"I appreciate your offer, but I am not going to take this position, I replied."

He is still my pastor and I love him very much.

The President

M y service and my waiting paid off—far greater that I had ever expected.

I was eventually promoted to serve in the position of Executive Vice President. I assisted with the day-to-day operations of the college. Dr. Chand and I were very close in age. I never thought that he would retire or even choose to change the direction of his life. I was settled with my role and secure in my support of his vision for the college.

I remember when Dr. Chand spoke with me about his desire to transition to a new role and new ministry opportunities. I was very surprised when he told me that he would recommend me the Board of Trustees and be appointed to serve as President of the college.

I had to talk with Esther. I needed to discuss the opportunity with her. We both had a lot of questions. Some questions were answered over time. Other answers became apparent as I began to prepare for the transition into the new role. Esther supported and encouraged me. "If that is what God is wanting you to do, I will support you," she said.

I wondered how the faculty, staff, and students would respond. Dr. Chand had been president for 14 years. He was very well known and respected. Would people respect me as the new president? Would they accept me? I felt overwhelmed as I pondered the awesome opportunity to serve. At times, I felt afraid. I was not afraid of leading, but of raising money and that I was to replace someone as popular and respected as Dr. Chand.

I faced many challenges as the time approached for the presentation to the Board of Trustees. How would I lead the team? My style of leadership is very different from Dr. Chand's. Would there be resentment? I needed to clearly articulate the vision and how that would be continued under my leadership. I believed in developing relevant Christian leaders for the ministry and the marketplace which is the mission of Beulah Heights Bible College. The vision to serve as a place of academic excellence, a resource center, and a change agent would not change. I asked God many times to give me wisdom.

I went to Nakuru with Dr. Chand before the Board meeting. During our stay, Dr. Chand announced his transition and my promotion to President. Applause erupted and the announcement received a standing ovation. I was overwhelmed by the confirmation and support of the people. I was one of them. They supported me. I received such affirmation. I knew from that moment that everyone was behind me. This was prior to Board approval and news traveled quickly to some of the staff and students. We quickly addressed some issues, but everything was handled smoothly and the transition began.

At my inauguration as president of Beulah Heights Bible College—hosted by North Avenue Presbyterian Church—senior pastor Dr. Scott Weimer spoke well of the school and how the people have supported our ministry. North Avenue Presbyterian Church has given 1. money and 2. thousands of dollars worth of equipment. They have a heart for missions and we have been able to work together.

At my inauguration, it was such a thrill for me to see Bishop Eddie Long stand in the pulpit at North Avenue Presbyterian Church. Bishop Long is the senior pastor of metro Atlanta's largest African-American church. At one point in the service, he stood hand in hand with my pastor. Other black pastors, such as Dr. Cynthia Hale and Dr. Wiley Jackson also participated. I was utterly amazed to see such a variety of ethnic leaders together.

Dr. Oliver Haney, an African-American leader attended my inauguration. He was the Dean at Interdenominational Theological Seminary (ITC) and later became their president. He is now chairman of the Board of Trustees at Beulah Heights Bible College. "That was incredible," "I have never witnessed such a thing before" he said.

More than 500 people attended my inauguration.

I would say 80 percent of them were African men, because of the students and other pastors who are more connected with the school.

For me, that was a dream come true. In fact, it was more than I had ever dreamed of achieving. Less than twenty years earlier I came to Atlanta as a student, lived in hardship, and now I reflect on what God has done in the years since that time.

Perhaps it is good to say, "Only in America could this have happened."

Where am I now? I see myself as a leader who has been able to bridge cultural and ethnic gaps. I see the college living up to the motto, "Breaking the mold and bridging the future."

I see it happening all around me. Who would have believed such camaraderie would exist among such diverse people? But it is happening and I believe it is only the beginning. Who knows what will happen during the next five years?

I had to overcome some intense obstacles. I struggled with the reality that I did not do things like Dr. Chand. And my style is different. I had to get my rhythm without breaking the dance. God finally helped me understand that I had to trust Him. I had to stop pulling people to myself. I did not want to impose. God reminded me that I can trust Him and let Him do things or I can do it myself. I chose to trust God.

As I have trusted God, I have watched Him work in the

midst of multiple lightning strikes, meeting the goal for accrediting body criteria, insurance and financial challenges, rate increases, and other numerous other obstacles.

People sometimes ask me, "Why did you stick it out at Beulah Heights? Why did you endure all the humiliation and rejection?" I stayed because I wanted to become a part of their history.

Primarily, I had a goal. I completed the program and continued on with my education. I resolved to discipline myself to God's direction and control. I had to trust Him.

Secondly, a Force—greater than myself—kept me here. With my education, I could have gone on to other organizations but I chose to remain. I did not feel free to go even when the offers were great. I had to follow God's leading.

Thirdly, I had determined in my own mind not to allow anything to derail me from my goals. I had sacrificed my business and so many things. Circumstances tried to diminish my will power but I was determined. I remembered that the treasure is within us and that patience pays. The Book of Wisdom tells us that.

Consider President George W. Bush. I see how focused he is on his agenda. He often speaks of it. Even though there are many things going on around him, he remains focused on his goals. He is an example of what it takes to stay focused.

God gives you the power to accomplish what He puts in your heart. I have learned that lesson from my personal experiences. As God deposits the dream, He provides the ability to accomplish it. If I could do it on my own, it would not be God's dream. As I think about all the things that I have come through to reach to this point in my life, I realize that it has been God providing the power to accomplish things larger than my dreams.

I was at Beulah Heights Bible College when only 80 students were enrolled. I have been through the whole process. When I first came, there was a strong possibility that the school would close. Each year the student intake was smaller. I was there when the change began. As soon as Sam Chand came in with fresh ideas and a willingness to work hard, things began to change. Under his leadership the school grew in every area. I feel privileged to have been chosen to carry on after him.

I was also there before his leadership began and during it. We worked hand-in-hand and shoulder-to-shoulder to build the school so that it received accreditation.

In some capacity, since I came to Beulah Heights Bible College I have been a part of the history. I feel as if it is my own house.

I learned a lot during my early days and some of those lessons came painfully. However, as I have grown I have learned that if we are faithful to follow the dream God plants in our hearts, He will work miracles.